The Way of the Rat

A *survival guide to office politics*

Joep P. M. Schrijvers

TRANSLATED BY JONATHAN ELLIS

CYANBOOKS

DISCLAIMER *Any resemblance to existing persons or organizations is purely coincidental. Should you recognize yourself in any of the anecdotes quoted here, don't worry: I meant somebody else.*

Copyright © 2004 Joep P. M. Schrijvers

Translation copyright © 2004 Scriptum

First published in Dutch as *Hoe word ik een rat? De kunst van het konkelen en samenzweren* by Scriptum, Schiedam, 2002

This translation first published in Great Britain in 2004 by Cyan Books, an imprint of

Cyan Communications Limited
Studio 4.3
The Ziggurat
60–66 Saffron Hill
London EC1N 8QX
www.cyanbooks.com

Reprinted in 2004, 2005

The right of Joep P. M. Schrijvers to be identified as the author of this work has been asserted by him in accordance with the Copyright, Designs and Patents Act 1988.

A CIP record for this book is available from the British Library

ISBN 0-9542829-2-2

Printed and bound in Great Britain by
TJ International, Padstow, Cornwall

"*And even thou, discerning one, art only a path and footstep of my will: verily, my Will to Power walketh even on the feet of thy Will to Truth!*"

Friedrich Nietzsche, *Thus Spake Zarathustra*

"*The two faculties belong together in so far as one of them, forgiving, serves to undo the deeds of the past, whose 'sins' hang like Damocles' sword over every new generation; and the other, binding oneself through promises, serves to set up in the ocean of uncertainty, which the future is by definition, islands of security without which not even continuity, let alone durability of any kind, would be possible in the relationships between men.*"

Hannah Arendt, *The Human Condition*

Contents

Preface

When I was 25, I reached a decision: I would spend the first half of my career in the heat of battle, and the second half in the peace and quiet of reflection. I have just soldiered through the first half and consider this book its proper conclusion. It's a typical hodgepodge: in part autobiographical, in part practical; sometimes critical, sometimes spiteful; here historical, there a glimpse of the future. People sometimes ask me whether I had an unhappy childhood or was traumatized by my work, and whether that explains why I lecture on the dirty tricks played in organizations. The answer is no. I had a happy childhood and I'm not in trauma. Anybody who reads this book carefully will understand my motives. You don't need a degree in psychology for that.

I would like to thank the many people who have played all these dirty tricks. The portrait of the rat that I paint in this book uses them as its model. I have spoken to several people who have confessed their "verminicity" to me. I have promised to respect their anonymity, so I won't mention their names here, but I would like to thank them sincerely for their honesty.

I would also like to thank Hans Janssen. He has been a constant source of encouragement, whether about giving lectures or writing this book. He provided me with contacts and, thanks to his considerable social flair, knew how to deal with my whims. I wrote this book in Germany, on a mountain. A very non-PC mountain, in a very non-PC place, near the very non-PC Berchtesgaden. A place like that makes you reflect on the lengths to which some rats go. My landlady, Ingrid Hellmiss, knew how to encourage me with a kind word and some overrich torte. And finally I would like to thank my friend Peter Heisterkamp for his sublime patience when my head was in the clouds, when I became so obsessed that I forgot everything, when I drifted off while he was telling me one of his stories (preferring to think about my own), and when I neglected to do the housework. Without his tolerance, this book would never have been written.

Joep Schrijvers
Summer 2004, Amsterdam

1 | **Welcome to the Sewer**

I'm a little hesitant about writing you this letter. On the one hand, I'm convinced that in times like these it's absolutely essential that you be told about the power plays that take place in organizations; on the other, I don't want to be judged as a ruthless consultant, a vindictive observer, or a cynical whistle-blower. I am, when all's said and done, just a person, and would like to be considered an ethical one at that. And yet I will be discussing what people call "screwing," "humiliating," "taking for a ride," and "victimizing."

We'll practice the art of undermining your boss; offer resistance to all those overpaid spreadsheet types who try to keep track of your every movement; and look at ways for you to manage your colleagues and fellow employees. So saddle up. We're going to explore the dark and devious ways of today's company.

As I mentioned, I'm writing this as a letter. I admit it's rather long. But that's because there is so much to tell you about the innards of a company. Traditionally, a letter is something to send to and receive from friends. The philosopher Sloterdijk* considers the letter as a metaphor for the way humanity has tried to humanize itself. Thanks to reading and writing, humanity has created a circle of learned people who have banded together to try to keep our animal instincts under control. Through a culture of books, essays, reviews, articles, stories, letters, and knowledge, humanity has tamed itself, and become a docile pet.

---

*Peter Sloterdijk, "Rules for the human park," a notorious lecture given in 1999. He suggested that humanization interventions have not improved mankind, and wondered whether we should not be considering genetic regulations. He was attacked for this, unjustly. He simply raised the question, and left the answer open.

Well, that may be a nice thought with which to go to sleep, but we know better. And I'm not even thinking about the atrocities that the human chimpanzee has perpetrated throughout the world. Even right here at home—in our own company, inside our own department, with our own clients— atrocities are committed every single day.

"Then why write a letter?" I hear you mutter. "It's so passé. Why not send an SMS or an email, or create a Web site? All those letters and books haven't done a thing to improve humanity." I'd have to agree with you. You're right.

And yet I'm still going to write what I want to tell you in the form of a letter. There's a simple reason. A letter is at once personal and distant, general and anecdotal; it exposes both the writer and the reader in all their imperfections and idiosyncrasies. And a letter between friends has a certain intimacy, one that we need if we're to discover how to be a rat.

Why "verminicity"?*

First of all, I'd like to explore the reasons why people play power games. But why should I want to do that in the first place?

The first reason that comes to mind is *sensationalism*. Be honest: can you really say you don't get a frisson of pleasure when you read that some high and mighty company president has been bettered by a lackey who's revealed a juicy bit of malpractice? How many of us follow the news—or even the soaps—to see how far the mighty have fallen? Who isn't amazed at all the wheeling and dealing that takes place at the top of companies? Who doesn't cringe at the ruthlessness of it all, or shiver at the cold calculations involved?

---

*OK, "verminicity" doesn't exist. Not as a word. But it does exist as an idea. I like to define it as "having the characteristics of vermin": creatures that are pests, in the sewers of cities and corporations.

You'd have to be made of concrete to withstand the thrill of someone else's downfall. Unfortunately, this excitement about dirty tricks at corporate or government level tends to be little more than the "Isn't that awful?" of village gossip.

And so, no matter how tempting sensation may be, I'm going to eschew it. If you're looking for juicy stories about big companies with cruel and fraudulent CEOs, I must disappoint you. I can't offer you anything like that. Perhaps you should subscribe to some glossy business magazine instead. Or purchase one of the "boy's own" books that describe the rise and fall of a big corporation as if it were a Greek tragedy. Such books are full of drama and tension. You get every detail about everybody and everything. Backstabbing and treachery set the tone. Exciting, isn't it?

My letter contains no infamous names or scandals, no revelations or exposés. That's quite deliberate; I am more interested in the rules of deviousness, the grammar of depravity, the structure of treachery. Sensationalism would prove too great a diversion from the matter in hand.

The second reason for turning the spotlight on verminicity could be the deep and satisfying feeling of *accusation*. Just imagine a book that, page after page, sharply and subtly exposes corporate intrigue in all its guises, juxtaposing fact with accusation: fault, people, fault, deed, fault.

I couldn't stand it. Why? The prosecutor is a bookkeeper, keeping precise track of everything that's right or wrong. Even worse, he knows exactly where the border between good and bad lies, where corporate integrity ends and verminicity begins. Such people despise tricks, coups, and whipping boys, whether their own or other people's. Prosecutors don't want to sully their hands—something that is inevitable once you enter the realms of management. And because they have a phobia for dirt, they want to clean up everything and everybody in their vicinity.

Prosecutors don't accuse other people; they accuse themselves. They stand alone in a dock of their own making, facing their own charges of secretly lusting after dirty tricks, sedition, coups, blackmail, and emotional cruelty. Let's be honest: anybody with clean hands has never really lived. The prosecutor lists his own offenses.

If I were to compose my letter on verminicity in this vein, the most I could produce is a sad, dull document all about me. And so you will find no accusations here. Nobody is on trial; nobody sets the standard.

Let's take a look at a third possible reason. It's a reason that many of my course participants have given at the start of my "How to be a rat" class. Yes, that's right: I've actually given courses in the subject. They often said: "I'm here because I want to be able to *recognize* what's going on and take steps to avoid it."

Idiots! I can still see their sorry faces now. With livid cheeks, sweat pouring from their armpits, and a nervous giggle, they signal exactly what they're going to ask. You hope for a miracle that will divert their words in a different direction, so that they'll say, "I really want to screw my boss," or "I'm really going after that one," or "I'm going to do everything I can—yeah, everything—to sabotage that team." You hope for a sniff of spite, a vapor of vengeance, a hunger for humiliation. But the words trip out so correctly: "I want to be able to recognize it and avoid it." And they are always so happy. Happy! You seldom see such frightened people so happy about giving the right answer. Because that answer puts them beyond suspicion. They're out of the firing line.

What they are really trying to say is that they don't want

anything to do with all this dirt; they just want to learn as many tricks as possible to strengthen their line of defense. They think that by doing this they'll keep their integrity and reduce their chance of victimization.

If you're looking for a book like that, look elsewhere. I could recommend a whole shelfful of do-it-yourself books that show you how to get along with your boss. These books give profiles of bosses and tips on how to keep them at arm's length. Often they are thinly disguised assertiveness courses.

In my letter, I want to go much further than that. I don't want you to keep on being the victim; I want to persuade you to get down in the dirt. Why shouldn't *you* become the boss from hell? One that is always calculating, weighing options, and circumnavigating pitfalls? One prepared to pick on inferiors and suck up to superiors whenever the opportunity arises?

Scientific research. Now there's a good reason for taking a long hard look at loutishness, cruelty, and dissembling. Our interest could be clinical; we are fascinated by the dark side of humanity, and have the urge to understand, explain, and predict it. Isn't that right?

We want to develop a neutral vocabulary to describe the traits we uncover. Neutral, because as scientific observers, as impartial onlookers, we simply want to plot the behavior of Homo sapiens; our preferences or disapproval are neither here nor there. We keep a measured distance from everyday language, freighted as it is with emotion, experience, and judgment. We observe depraved managers and their employees in their natural habitat, their organizations, to discover under what circumstance which form of loutishness is adopted, by which person, to what end.

We try to find patterns in their political behavior, and label them laws. Example? All managers eventually act like jerks, even the nicest and most sympathetic. The reason is that acting like a jerk is part of the unwritten law to which a manager will conform.* Of course, we choose neutral terms, scientific terms, and we describe the law as follows: "Managers give priority to the interests of the organization in those situations where a conflict of interest can occur. The reason for this prioritizing is inherent in the role as perceived by those in a leadership function."

There is nothing really wrong with the scientific approach. Quite the opposite. The neutralization of language and strict control over subjectivity and personal preferences have brought to light things that would otherwise have remained hidden. No, things go wrong when people—professionals—make use of such scientific language in their everyday environment. What you get then is intellectual drivel.

Intellectual drivel

It's exactly this intellectual drivel that is the real reason why we should concern ourselves with verminicity. I should explain.

One of the biggest mistakes we make is to use scientific jargon to describe how we obstruct our boss and exclude our colleagues. We then fall into the same pit that has claimed so many professionals during high-school education, university, and any number of training courses. In all these contexts, they are extensively schooled in the use of the neutral vocabulary of scientific disciplines.

Much of today's professional training is little more than language training. People suddenly start coming out with such

---

*Loek Schönbeck, *Oneerbiedige wijsbegeerte van het management* [*Irreverent Philosophy of Management*], Scriptum, Schiedam, 2001. A highly readable book, which reveals how modern organizations use language as camouflage—and a breath of fresh air after all the management and leadership guff of the 1990s.

terms as "paradigms," "step plans," "typologies," "action plans," "audits," "governance models," and the like. This use of language may be a blessing and an enrichment for the scientist, but it often proves a curse and an impoverishment for the layperson.

Objective language removes all emotion and nuance from the actions that people initiate. In other words, they use the language of an observer to describe their actions as participants. Yet they are not flies on the wall but active participants in social intercourse—eh, sorry—people with vices, lusts, grievances, and fears. You shouldn't use scientific vocabulary in such circumstances; you should use the language of the factory floor, the language of the cafeteria, the language of gossip. In other words, the language you use at home when you're pissed with your job: *that* language.

This quasi-scientific terminology has given discussions about professional practice a veneer of respectability. It has cloaked them in the veil of innocence. It has washed the blood from the walls, swept the filth off the doorstep, and papered over the deviousness. Professional training is nothing more than learning the vocabulary of propriety: how to speak politely and use your knife and fork correctly.

But does this mean that our organizations have become extremely proper? Have we driven out every vestige of vileness and cruelty? Has the great humanization process finally kicked in?

No. At some point in their careers, professionals realize they've been taken in by intellectual drivel. Sure, they have an arsenal of neat, polite professional models, but they're faced with a day-to-day existence that's light years away. It grates and groans; nothing fits anymore. It's a painful position to be in, and many try to worm themselves out of it. Do they succeed? Can they really escape? No. They can't.

Most professionals simply turn into schizos. They lead a double life. They use the pretty words that a company expects to hear. They mouth phrases about "openness and honesty," "commitment," "synergy," and yet they know that top management always keeps essential information to itself, that personnel say one thing in the cafeteria and another in meetings, and that everybody fences in their own little backyard.

At home, they moan and groan. They say what they really feel: the boss is a pig, the department is arrogant, employees think only about themselves, and they are still years away from the financial security they need. I certainly wouldn't want to change places with professionals who have chosen this route.

Another group of professionals turn into happiness junkies. They search for intellectual salvation in the piles of self-help books and a plethora of expensive seminars and conferences. And they learn all about healing methods that, if followed correctly, will work wonders for their organization.

They learn how to set goals and design action plans, and how to achieve them without hurting anybody else. Or they learn some new typology of people, with all the associated sets of characteristics. "If you adapt yourself to the whims of the other person, you'll see that things will go really smoothly." Or they'll discover that people have a dark side, and they'll start calling it a "trap."

Talk about prissiness! "Your opportunistic and sado-masochistic cruelty is a real trap for you." Just imagine all those managers with responsibility for millions of dollars saying, "You have a trap." Bah! Then they learn that you have to help somebody get out of the trap. And the way to do that is first of all to understand their own traps.

They end up with the gurus who know everything about happiness: happy workers, happy bosses, happy clients, happy shareholders, happy bankers. No more distrust, no more backstabbing and manipulation, as long as you follow the 12, 20, or 50 steps. You and everybody else.

Hmm. What I don't understand is: if happiness is there for the taking and if it can be captured methodically—at least if we believe the prophets—then why don't I see it all around me? Ever met a happy employee? A manager with integrity? A self-motivated and smiling colleague? No! The only happy people are the prophets who spread the message. Who wouldn't be happy with so many disciples and followers?

Everything would be all right if it went no further, if these prophets were simply quacks. But the situation is far more serious than we imagine. Their methods are not just ineffectual, they actually make things worse. They increase the pain. The chasm becomes wider. We get more of the same.

There's only one way to make the drivel bearable. Because we'll never be able to get ourselves completely out of the painful position we're in. And the solution is simple; very simple. From today, we stop pushing everyday reality through the grinder of propriety. It doesn't help; it leads nowhere; it's a dead end. No, from now on we'll confine ourselves to normal language. The language of jealousy, cruelty, hate, anger, coldness, and power. Language that bewitches, humiliates, defiles. The language of villains; the language of rats!

REFINED LANGUAGE	NEUTRAL LANGUAGE	RAT LANGUAGE
• Serving leader	• Manager	• Boss
• Coaching	• Showing leadership	• On your back
• Inspire	• Motivate	• Manipulate
• Colleague	• Actor	• Bastard
• Trap	• Weakness	• Loutishness
• Motivation	• Interest	• Lining your pockets

REFINED LANGUAGE	NEUTRAL LANGUAGE	RAT LANGUAGE
• Results-oriented	• Forceful	• Domineering
• Committed	• Doing your job	• Crawling
• Procedures	• Actions	• Tricks
• Mission	• Business plan	• Garbage
• Strength	• Influence	• Power
• Issue	• Problem	• Can of worms

The language of the rat

In this book, we'll try to use the language of the villains: those we call "opportunists," because they calculate, make plans, and strike. This creates unease, resistance, and disbelief. Do people who are so rotten truly exist? Oh yes. Loads of them.

"So explain why adopting rat language, rather than refined or neutral language, should make the divide between experience and the sanitized view of our professional activities less painful. If the result is such a mix of emotions and reactions, won't it just make things worse?"

Yes. But only for those people who like happy books and delusions. Only they will object. They'll get confused and, in a knee-jerk reflex, reach for the familiarity of their sweet little words. But for those who have the courage to peel away their scabs and look the demon company directly in the eye, and for those who dare to take the next step and join the ranks of those who consider themselves rats, a new game will emerge that will take them to a new level of perception. They'll find a soothing poultice to draw out the pus of intellectual drivel. In this letter, I offer you cold compresses, splints, and warm blankets.

We'll bridge the gap between pretty words and everyday practice by discussing the question: how to be a rat. That's the ultimate reason for this book. The emergence of the rat is another story altogether.

Emergence

A few years ago, I was involved in a large reorganization of middle and higher professional education. It involved the introduction of new teaching methods, new material, new administration forms, mergers, and alternative means of governmental funding. I had the role of project manager, which meant I spent hours sitting at a table with board members, principals, course developers, human resources managers, and PR specialists trying to channel the conversation in a productive way.

During that time, I ran up astronomical telephone bills and drank gallons of coffee. I soon realized that everybody was as open as a recalcitrant oyster, and as personally involved with daily affairs as a shareholder is with workers. Everybody had, tucked away somewhere, a personal agenda, an unpaid bill. And the battle was anything but friendly.

I recall dealing with a school principal. He had to merge with another school, and had carefully selected three potential brides with whom to make the best possible marriage. Nothing wrong with that. Then I discovered that the good man was interested only in obtaining the best—rather, the highest—possible position in the new organization. Nothing wrong with that, either.

So what made this man a rat? What made him an example to us? He had carefully assessed the dowry he would have to pay. He told me in an unguarded moment at the end of one of our meetings: "I'll be the rector. And I've agreed with them that I'll get rid of half my staff. Then we'll merge. That'll save a lot of money. I can easily get rid of them now. Save a lot of unwanted ballast. The other schools already have too many staff. If I brought all of mine with me, the situation would be impossible. So, in exchange, I want the job of rector. It's up to them: either I bring everybody with me and assume a minor role, or save a lot of money and secure a plum job for me. Life is all about choices."

Yes—life is all about choices. I drove home with mixed feelings: admiration for such cunning calculation, anger with myself for my naiveté, and disbelief ... I believe that was the very first time I ever whispered to myself: "What a rat! People like this are much more interesting than all those wimpy organization advisers who go around preaching corporate salvation." I've met a lot more rats since then. You can spot them easily with a trained eye.

Some time later, I went to an introductory meeting about a new job. That afternoon, I'd had talks with a man who had held a whole set of knives to my throat. He wanted this, he wanted that. With the adrenaline still pumping through me and in great haste, I arrived at the departmental meeting with my future colleagues. When they asked me what I'd been doing recently, I could only answer: "I've been dealing with rats. Rats in all shapes and sizes. Male rats, female rats. Good rats and evil rats. And do you know what the difference is between them?"

Silence.

"No? You don't recognize a good rat for the rat he is. You only recognize a bad rat. A good rat doesn't boast about his tricks, about the master strokes he's pulled off. I'm a bad rat. Rats look as normal as anybody else. They don't have long eyelashes or strange lumps on their heads or scars down their cheeks. They look like every other father and mother taking care of their children in a neat suburb. Take a look at the person next to you. They could be a rat. They could be hatching evil plans. They could be plotting against you and everybody else."

My new colleagues looked at each other, then back at me, and burst out laughing.

And it was then that I thought to myself: "I should give a course in how to be a rat, and talk about all the tactics and tricks a rat uses." It was another two years before I summoned the courage, the time, and the inclination to develop it.

One day, when business was a little slow, I thought, "Now's the time to plan the course." I opened my laptop, created a new document entitled "rat lesson plan," and started, as a good course developer should, to write down a whole list of aims: at the end of this workshop, the participant should be capable of analyzing the arenas, choosing rat techniques, and employing them ....

Just then the telephone rang. "This is M—— at the University of X——. I'm calling to see whether you would be willing to give a talk at a seminar we're organizing for our graduates. They feel they are all under the thumbs of the professors. They are being used. Would you stick up for them?"

They want me to prosecute, I thought. They want me to deliver a *j'accuse*. What a coincidence that I should at this very moment be thinking about a course dealing with political manipulation in companies!

"M——," I said, "I really don't feel like moaning and gnashing my teeth with a group of students. It will only confirm them in their role of victim. That's no good to anybody. But I have developed a course [*white lie!*] called 'How to be a rat.' Wouldn't that be of interest to your graduates? Then you can train them in the fine art of undermining and victimizing their professors and superiors. How does that sound? By the way, do you know how to make a whipping boy? I can tell you how to do that as well."

M—— burst out laughing, and seemed interested. We got down to business. I had exactly four weeks to get everything ready. Then I drove down south to teach my first pupils how to live in the sewer. I didn't realize then that I would travel quite a lot in the future to give these courses. And I certainly didn't think I would be writing you a letter about it, telling you all about the rat in its many guises.

A quick tour of the sewer

I'll be dealing with a number of issues in the rest of this letter. For your convenience, I'll run through them quickly now.

An audit The first section of the letter contains a self-test. Most professionals are familiar with personality tests. You'll have seen things like: "What sort of leader am I?" "What personality type am I?" "Should I be more target-focused?" "Do I have what it takes to succeed?"

My letter wouldn't be complete without such a test. And so I'll be giving you plenty of opportunity to assess yourself in the next section of this letter. You will, of course, appreciate that the test is highly scientific and carefully tuned, so you should respect the results. Even more important than the results are the statements I've used to sum up the right sort of attitude for a rat. More on this later.

In the arena Some people are a bit disappointed that a rat must spend so much time observing and so little time actually doing anything. But that's how it is. Good rats will attack only three times a month, for up to five minutes a time. But they know that when they *do* attack, victory is assured. And they celebrate their victory in silence, never mentioning it to anybody.

In this part, we take a look at organizational arenas. People who know the battlegrounds are better prepared than their opponents. The most difficult part here is to identify the people involved. We'll take a look at the competing interests within the company.

And if after this section you still think you can't do anything, you should just forget about the rest of this letter.

The sources of power *Everybody* has power. And everybody has sources of power. Unfortunately, not everybody is able to access these sources with the same ease. The art is to push ahead with the power you have, and get some of the power you don't have.

We'll be looking at the strength of the monopoly. And what about all those possibilities offered by the organization and its procedures? You have more opportunities for tormenting others than you imagine. And don't underestimate your body: there's a lot of power there too. If you want to dive deeper into things, you should take a look at the possibilities of "Big Brother" forms of suppression. They are a unique source of various facilities and surprising opportunities. I'll also be talking about a power source that anybody can access: friends, the network. And I'll end with the art of sorcery, because anybody who doesn't know how to cast a spell will never do well in the arena.

Tricks and ruses Ever since Machiavelli, countless lists have been drawn up detailing the golden "dos and don'ts" for the ruthless ruler. In this letter from the gutter, I'll take a look at the most important tactics used by the rat.

We'll deal with the importance of concealing your true nature. A good rat is never recognized as such. And we now know the same is true of terrorists. The most evil people live normal and respectable lives, rid themselves of any traits that might show them for what they are, and then emerge unexpectedly for their five-minute assault ...

We'll also look at the microtactics that can be used at a

moment's notice. Just to give you a taste for what's to come, we'll be talking about how to draw up a front in the department and how best to play one colleague off against another. We'll talk about subversion tactics. How do you get rid of a manager? How do you sabotage a boss that gets your goat? Read on, and be amazed how simple these tactics are. There's so much to say about the manipulative person.

Did you know that the highest level of verminicity is to make yourself unpredictable, so that neither your boss nor your colleagues ever know which way you'll turn? It sends them crazy, and that gives you the chance to turn their mistakes to your advantage. This is where the bureaucratic work of the rat comes in.

A lot of the rat's work involves using others' weakness to his or her own advantage. This is where the rat differs from the therapist. Therapists are expected to manipulate you for your own good. That's not what we are about. If you want to be a good rat, you must learn to sniff out the hidden desires and fears of your opponent.

Gracián, a Jesuit priest to the Spanish court, wrote some 400 years ago that a made-to-measure thumbscrew could be produced for everybody.* It's true; everybody has a weak spot, a whim, a nasty habit, a quirk, a childish fear, or a phobia—something that undermines their autonomy and makes them dependent on the outside world. When you can become that outside world, you have them in your power. Controlling weaknesses, controlling fear—that's not at all difficult. All you have to do, as I'll explain, is follow two rules.

---

*See Baltasar Gracián, *The Art of Worldly Wisdom*, Shambhala Publications, Boston, Mass., 2004. A beautifully written life philosophy, still appropriate today.

The bigger picture Is there anything more satisfying than moving step by step toward the aims you've set yourself: taking over the company, playing your competing colleagues offside, subverting the boss, or seizing the initiative? But something like that demands a full appreciation of the fine art of conspiracy and collusion.

You'll have to decide whether you are passive or reactive. You'll have to consider the opening gambit, the middle game, the moment of truth, and the final thrust. You'll have to think about which card you should play and when. And which cards you still need. Timing is the most difficult part of the rat's game plan.

If you really want to engage in a fine battle, a struggle for life and death, then inevitably the moment of truth will arrive. And what we all hope is that we've planned everything down to the last detail, overlooked nothing, anticipated every event, and prepared the cleverest move ever played.

And yet you can still lose. Yours was the weaker hand. You weren't devious enough. Or you ran out of luck. What then? Do you have the noblesse oblige of the defeated rat? Do you dare turn your back on your company, surrender your status, face the prospect of selling a street newspaper to your ex-colleagues, and confine your luxury shopping to Wal-Mart? If such prospects don't bother you, you'll be strong in the rat game.

But promise me one thing: if the battle is about something really important and you lose, you must leave, resign, start again—but *never stay*. Because if you do, the victors will treat you like shit on their shoes.

Surfing to tradition In this section, I'll be dealing with a number of highlights in the history of power. All the tricks we use now are part of a long tradition, and I think professionals should be aware of their roots. But there's more to it than that.

First, knowledge alleviates loneliness. You come to understand that others have wrestled with similar problems and formulated responses to them.

Second, the tradition consists of an accumulation of fertile and sterile thoughts, ideas, and techniques. You meet them in proverbs, parables, fables, metaphors, urban myths, and the like. You are always part of the collective competence and incompetence. Tradition is a bit like the Internet: you can find everything there, ripe and ready for harvesting. Knowledge sets you free. You can reject, embrace, or recycle tradition; you can never pretend it doesn't exist.

And finally, knowledge of your roots makes your political intrigues more adaptable. You find an ever-increasing number of options for your actions; more than enough reasons to take a short trip through the highlights of political dealings.

Epilogue And finally, I've written a short epilogue. In it, I sum up the contents of my letter.

And that's the way the story will be told.

Take care
Before you move on to the self-test, a few remarks about the structure of this letter from the gutter.

Precautionary measures As you read this book, you'll meet all sorts of people: the bastard boss, that prick of a colleague, the snitch. If your adrenaline levels rise, that's fine. That's the way it should be. Physical excitement is vital. After all, Schopenhauer located the will in the body.

And yet you must refrain from submerging yourself in your wounded pride, your appetite for destruction, or your animal aggression. That could be dangerous. Intellect must prevail at all times. That's why you should take some precautionary measures: arrange regular spells of loneliness in which you can reflect on your situation; distance yourself from email and cellphone babble; find a buddy with whom you can scheme and hatch plans; or develop a fine sense of irony, self-deprecation, and exaggeration. Camp is an excellent method of combating the dark side in others, and in yourself. I've had good experience with this approach myself.

Disclaimers Over the years, many people have confessed their intrigues to me, whether great or small. I'll tell you about some of them when I consider it necessary. But I've made them anonymous and untraceable to protect the interests of those who put their trust in me. And, as I've already explained, I'm more interested in the nature of verminicity than in exposing yet another scandal (though I must admit the temptation was sometimes hard to resist). So any resemblance to existing managers, board members, trade union officials, shareholders, and assorted scum is purely coincidental.

I'm assuming that you are mentally healthy, know yourself pretty well, and are fully aware of what you do or don't want. So you must accept full responsibility for any actions you may undertake after you've read this book; the author can't be held accountable for any of them. Don't bother complaining to me if you are fired or sued, or if your husband throws you out; I shall always maintain this was never intended to be a serious book.

Welcome to the sewer.

2 | **The Audition**

After the overture in the previous section, it's about time to introduce the main subject. We can't put it off any longer, even though I understand all the reasons you may have for wanting to do just that. The prospect of examining yourself in the mirror and reaching the conclusion that you are not an innocent, or worse, that you are a conniving bastard, is far from pleasant. The self-image you have built up with such care over the years —I am a sharp person, I am a person of integrity—may have to be drastically revised.

But be comforted: for most people, the fear of living a lie is greater than the pain of living with a terrible truth. And that's why tests, audits, and assessments enjoy such incredible popularity. So to satisfy this need, I have developed a self-test, and I'll now ask you to submit to it—willingly.

I've kept the test simple, and modeled it on the sort of thing that regularly appears in glossy magazines. You know what I mean: are you a dominant character? Could you be a good leader? Are you a born adviser? Are you the perfect lover? And so on.

Although most of these tests have as much value as a horoscope, tarot card, or palm reading—in other words, none at all—you'll understand that my test is of a completely different and altogether superior order. It will reveal the knowledge that you've been seeking about yourself for so long: the knowledge about your verminicity.

Those who have been able to resist the temptation of such tests thus far may need instructions:

THE WAY OF THE RAT

- Read the statement carefully.
- Respond quickly with an intuitive "yes" or "no."
- Add up the numbers for each question.
- Determine your score.

The test

	Yes A	No B
1. *I really enjoy participating in political games in my company*	2	0
2. *I always carefully assess the interests involved in and around my work*	2	1
3. *I understand how my company's "court" works*	2	1
4. *I am good at interrogating and interviewing*	3	1
5. *I always know where I'm going. I know my aims*	2	0
6. *I always plan three steps ahead*	3	1
7. *I know exactly which power sources I can tap*	2	1
8. *I frequently reveal everything I know and feel*	0	3
9. *I always look for the other person's weak spot*	4	1
10. *I'm scared of losing*	1	3
11. *I object to office politics. One has to be open and honest!*	1	3
12. *I hate creating victims*	0	2
13. *The ends justify the means*	2	1
Total A:		B:
Total: A + B		

If you want to know what sort of rat you are, turn to the results on page 49.

The statements
Let's go through each of the statements included in the self-test and see what goes to make up a conspirator's core competence,

and how it contributes to success or failure. After all, we'll need to marinate ourselves in all the elixirs of opportunistic wisdom if we are to take on their rich, deep flavors.

I really enjoy participating in political games in my company

When I held the position of manager in an IT company, responsible for 25 programmers, I'd often talk to them about their ambitions, the profession, and the activities they undertook for their clients. Most of them had been working for about three years and had already undergone their initiation into corporate life.

When I asked them what they wanted to be, most of them would answer "a manager," a smaller number would say "a consultant," and a very few nerds would say "working in technology." And when I asked them what they disliked most about their work, the number one answer—well, number one after "traveling time"—was "all that political stuff." Those upstairs—the bosses—were always colluding, catching each other off guard, setting ambushes for each other, and protecting their own personal interests, while all the time pretending that their heart and soul were in the company.

When I pointed out that a considerable amount of a manager's time is spent in "all that political stuff"—that that's what you get paid for, and that political acuteness is part of the job description, or, at the very least, of the manager's core competence—they would fall silent. Occasionally, I would see someone's eyes light up when they suddenly realized that "all that political stuff" was part of life and you could actually get some enjoyment from it. Mostly, though, I would see the same dull eyes as always. It's a lost cause, I would think; they'll never get far as a rat.

Anybody who realizes that all that political stuff is part of

31

life and can actually be enjoyable sharpens their eyes, experiments, and develops the sensitivity that is so vital in a rat's life.

I always carefully assess the interests involved in and around my work

Have you ever noticed how people become disturbed when personal interests are mentioned, even though they are part and parcel of negotiations between employers and trade unions? Apparently, there are certain areas where you may talk in terms of interests, and others where this is strictly off limits. Why is that, and what does it mean for the rat?

The only explanation I can give is that a company likes to preserve the illusion that it is a dedicated battalion that marches forward, united in common purpose, to seize the market and hold everything together. I use military terms because that's the sort of language managers like to use. They see their company as a fighting unit—one that has rid itself of internal differences and rivalries, unless these can bring the ultimate victory nearer.

In many companies, you witness interventions aimed at strengthening feelings of unity and sharing, and stamping out internecine warfare. "We are this type of company." "This is our mission." "These are the foundations of our culture." "These are our values." If you're very lucky, you'll be given a pretty little book devised by some clever PR agency or other. They may even send you a T-shirt with a logo that epitomizes togetherness.

All this unifying rhetoric is nothing more than refined language calculated to muddy the differences between "thine" and "mine." The language of interests is sobering, and can be disconcerting, but it brings relationships back to basics: this is my interest, and this is yours.

I'd like to make one observation here. We mustn't allow ourselves to drift back into the old class war where the boss was always the bad guy who stuck it to everybody, and the employee was always the good guy who ended up slinking away with his tail between his legs. Reality, thankfully, is somewhat more subtle.

Most employees are fully aware of their interests: their position and status, so much money for winter sport, their place in the hierarchy, where they might end up, the little beach hotel they want to run, at least one sabbatical. In these lists, the interests that have a direct bearing on the company are conspicuous by their absence.

So it's even more amazing that employees wipe this "thine" and "mine" from their brain the instant they log on at their designer desk (after first, of course, exchanging the latest gossip at the coffee machine). All at once, they become cosseted in the perfume of loyalty to the company, in the warmth of the imagined involvement of bosses, directors, and CEO.

Let me say one thing: rats are always totally committed to their own interests. And any other interest—whether of colleagues, professional friends, the bosses, the shareholders, or the customer—is only valued in so far as it contributes to or detracts from their own interests. A symbiotic relationship between company and employee is utterly alien to a rat.

I understand how my company's "court" works

Any company of any size—let's say, with at least five employees —has a clique that discusses strategy fights the fight, and shares out the spoils. Every company has its own "court": the people who cluster around the center of power; the fruit flies buzzing around the directors, the CEO, the founders, and the main shareholders. They are the courtiers with whom the powerful share some, if not all, of their problems.

To avoid any misunderstanding, I should say that the court doesn't necessarily reflect the company's formal hierarchy. Somebody far removed from the top may still, at a given moment, be elevated to minor royalty and be allowed to enter the throne room to shake up the cushions. At the same time, somebody near the top may be excluded from any confidences, simply because he or she poses a threat to the monarch.

One characteristic of a court is that it is faithful to the management and would never pull any stunts. In exchange for this loyalty, members are afforded a range of privileges, such as increased freedom, rewards, inside information, and praise. In that respect, the court of our present-day corporate life is little different to the courts of the duchies and principalities of Machiavelli's day.

You can make good use of the court as long as you understand exactly how it works. Let's describe the various functions in some detail.

First, the nobles of the company are the bosses' eyes and ears. Nothing more, nothing less. They are expected to observe what's going on among employees, managers, and the outside world. Anything that can't be processed by the monthly management information reports—so-called "soft" information, in other words—is provided by the company's dukes and countesses. In informal conversations, when they "wrangle" with their boss, when they "catch up" on things, when they "collaborate" over ideas, they warn, support, and encourage their sires and, on the odd occasion, carefully and politely contradict them.

Second, the nobles act as sparring partners. Ideas are launched for them first, so that they can either shoot them down or wish them Godspeed. The subjects vary from person to person, of course, but the standard agenda generally contains the following matters:

- Direction of the company
- Acquisition and sales of shares
- Recalcitrant staff
- Fear of working in different directions
- Introduction of mega changes
- Resistance in the organization.

And if you reach the position of true confidant, which seldom happens with your own boss, then they will also discuss with you:

- No longer interested in being the boss
- Why haven't I made my fortune yet?
- How can I get rid of my director?

You'll now understand that the court is an invaluable source of information for anybody wanting to be a rat.

You may be asking how you can become part of the court if you don't already belong to it. The simplest method is to lick your way into the good books of some lower member. Because what do the lower members of the court need most? You've got it—their own court! Even if it's tiny, perhaps just a couple of people.

When I was a manager, I had two people with whom I would speak in confidence. I had allowed myself a small court, created my eyes and ears in the department, and selected my sparring partners, my confidants. Neither of them was vitriolic or a nag; they didn't mind rolling up their sleeves; and, most important, they were genuinely concerned about ups and downs. In exchange for acting as my courtiers, they knew earlier than anybody else what was in the pipeline for them and others, enjoyed greater freedom in their work, and were given better opportunities to shine at internal and external gatherings.

I am good at interrogating and interviewing

You must know people who always manage to get you to tell them more than you were planning to. People who, with genuine or feigned innocence, approach you, break down all your defenses, roll themselves up into a cute little ball, and let you talk, occasionally making an encouraging remark or nodding their understanding as a reward for your openness. These people should be an example to us; we must make their ability our own.

How do you define the noble art of interrogation, and why is it part of the essential armory of anybody wishing to rule the roost? To answer the second question first, good rats are always gathering information. They already have many of the pieces of the puzzle in their heads, and want to complete the picture. They want to piece things together so that they can say: "I see. Now I understand what they're playing at."

Documents, snippets of gossip, emails, back corridors, confidences—rats use them all to formulate their ideas, queries, suspicions, and then use their methods to identify and exploit any ambiguities. They know what they're looking for—and where to find it.

This is something that talented consultants, diplomats, ambassadors, and leaders have always done, and will continue doing. And if they aren't sure about exactly what they need to know, they can always feign interest and get the other person talking.

Interrogation is a simple ability, and it can be learned in a most pleasant way: in the bar. But let me first elaborate on the technique.

The key is to stop doing one of the things you've been trained to do (and the biggest load of nonsense that the hordes of communication experts have ever thought up): you must stop listening. Because 80% of what people say is nothing more than an excuse for exercising their vocal cords. All you need to do is catch the adjectives a person uses.

"The meeting was chaotic." Let's suppose that's what somebody tells you. What you then have to do is to interrogate them about the adjective "chaotic." What you must *not* do is ask whether it was the fault of the chairman or the agenda. That is fundamentally wrong, because the information you need is contained in the word "chaotic." All you have to do is repeat it and turn it into a question. "Chaotic?" "Yes," the other person will then say, "because those two just kept on going at each other …"

And so our informant reveals exactly what we want to know: the world behind the scenes, the meaning behind the meaning, the agenda behind the agenda. Go to the bar every night for three weeks and interrogate somebody different each time. Ask them about their youth, their work, their sex lives, their finances—but do it by observing the adjectives. You'll be amazed at what you get to know in thirty minutes.

I always know where I'm going. I know my aims
You may say that this speaks for itself; how foolish of me to introduce such an obvious statement at this point in my letter. I confess to a certain embarrassment, because I don't wish to bore you with platitudes. And yet it's essential to stress that you should set your own goals and know exactly where you are going no matter what arena you are playing in.

Tell me, do you really know your aims, apart from getting through the week? Could you list them for me without having to think about them? Probably not. Most professionals couldn't either. Their mouths simply fall open when you ask them.

You need aims, because they give you an instrument for

determining your strategy and planning your tactics. There's a huge difference between wanting to get promoted quickly and wanting to get the best out of an early retirement scheme. Your strategy and your moves will be different. If you don't have aims, being a rat is rather pointless.

Many companies today encourage employees to develop their own personal development plan (PDP), or individual development plan (IDP), or career development plan (CDP). They are even given training in this by some HRM bitch or other elegantly educated sucker.

Remember one rule: your aims are yours and yours alone. Nobody else has any right to know about them. Your boss isn't open about his or her aims, so I recommend you keep yours private and confine your PDP to trivial matters. PDPs are used by companies to formulate their own aims, which may not coincide with yours. What's more, if you talk about your aims too much, your opponents will be able to anticipate your actions.

Know your aims, but talk about them as little as possible, unless it suits your plans. And take the P out of the PDP.

I always plan three steps ahead

Every one of today's professionals has undergone massive training in long-term strategy and learned all about models and step plans. Yet most of them can't think beyond today's lunch appointment. Sure, they have plans, but they are seldom able to explain how these plans relate to the current climate or the company's present-day situation.

Yet this is something a good politician can easily master. Determine now what the next three steps could be. What will happen if I do this? And what will I do if somebody else does that? And what ... ? Not only is the "what if" method suitable for analyzing scenarios, but it can also help you anticipate possible results.

I believe many professionals find this difficult because although they have the intellectual prowess needed to design a step plan, they lack the imagination to visualize how a power play might develop from the current situation. Anybody who combines analytical ability with imaginative insight can gain a distinct advantage in any power play.

To help you think ahead, it's useful to divide the game into three sections: opening, middle, and end game. Every battle, every coup, every conspiracy follows this pattern, and each section has its own function and dynamics.

In the opening, the players have to set out their aims and secure the best starting position. The middle game is about collecting as many trump cards as possible to use at the moment of truth: the point when the middle game progresses to the end game. All that remains then is the fighting. In the opening game you have to take into account the middle game and make sure the points are set in the right direction for the end game. We'll discuss this in more detail later.

I know exactly which power sources I can tap

It is rare for somebody in a company to be apathetic, paralyzed, and trapped with no room for maneuver. Every single employee possesses sources of power that can help them make their work, their department, and, yes, even their boss dance to their tune. In some companies, ingenious maneuverings and uses of sources of power have enabled employees to topple seemingly impregnable top managements by exposing their words, deeds, and emotional tyranny.

You generally have two such sources of power within easy reach: the power of delay and the power of the network.

To take the first one first: many people have tapped this source and, by careful calculation, managed to prevent all sorts of disaster. How? Simply by saying, loudly and without hesitation, a resounding "No!"

Some people find the weapons of delay embedded in laws and regulations. By using them, such people have been able to delay—often for years on end—the building of a new tunnel or a new rail link. Others are more creative. They plant trees in places earmarked for runways. Or they sell off land in tiny parcels to as many people as possible in the hope that the expropriation process won't be able to cope. Others delay trains so that the management fails to reach the punctuality targets it has set itself, and has to slink off to some other position. Everybody can use the power of delay. But I should point out that adopting these tactics doesn't as yet lead to you achieving the goals you've set for yourself.

For that you need more. You must find people to become part of your network, and cherish them. That automatically brings me to the second source of power, namely the people you know in and outside the company. Your network is where you pick up the latest news, identify the hobbyhorses, meet the influencers, rub elbows with the decision makers, and find inspiration.

One of the most powerful women I have ever met in Holland had built up her power in this way. She was a networking genius. At the height of her career she knew everybody, sharing tables with top functionaries, CEOs, artists, business executives, and trade unionists. How did she do it? She had a good nose for people who matter, she could assume a mantle of vulnerability (appreciated by everybody), and estimate the current and future value of anybody (not appreciated by everybody).

Anyone who wants to achieve anything must fill their electronic agenda to the absolute limit. Delay and networking are key tools for a rat.

I frequently reveal everything I know and feel

Most books about power and politics praise silence as a noble virtue. Yet in a culture that preaches unconditional openness and honesty, and tries to persuade us that business and personal success depend on them, the idea of being guarded, of developing an acute understanding of what we should and shouldn't say, can often seem like an anachronism.

You don't like your boss? Then tell her. You don't like your team? Be upfront with them. Is your customer a pain in the neck? Let him know about it. Kings must behave majestically. Modern professionals don't let things eat them up from inside.

All the same, many professionals learn from bitter experience that it's better to remain silent on crucial issues. The result can be seen in so many organizations: the comedy of open communications. People who follow their emotions, promote their interests, air their displeasure about what's going on, and complain in the corridors, cafeterias, and even at home about so-and-so—people like that soon find themselves kicked upstairs because they have dared to tell things as they are.

So many organizations today proudly proclaim their openness in their annual report, trumpet it in corporate presentations, fill their walls with it in gaudy technicolor, as if to say that here, in this place, openness and honesty are hallowed; here, there is a culture of trust. Avoid these companies like the plague! Such displays are nothing more than a public yearning for what's missing: honesty and openness. You've entered a place where it is dangerous to show what you think and feel.

For the moment, I'll simply quote Gracián, our Spanish confessor. His 148th aphorism says: "Have the art of conversation, for it is the hallmark of the man. No human enterprise demands greater heed, for [it makes up] so large a part of everyday life, whence its dangers, or its advantages."*

I always look for the other person's weak spot

A good rat will develop the ability to create a "psychogram" of another person in a flash. And he or she pays particular attention —as does a psychotherapist—to the aberrations in that person's character. It is these traits that make the other weak, threaten his or her autonomy, and promote dependency on others. And it is exactly this dependency that interests us, since it affords us the chance of taking control. Everybody has a weak spot, a bad habit, a vice, or a character blemish. We must expose it and use it to our advantage.

A therapist makes use of the darker side of someone's character for that person's own good; rats do it in their own interests. Professionals who have enjoyed training in ethics and good practice will have to make a minor adjustment that they will experience as a major freedom. They can finally become what they have always secretly believed themselves to be: merciless manipulators.

For years they have made use of the fear, pride, ambition, childish desire, and lust of others. And they have, until now, called this "motivating," "inspiring," "committing," and "challenging." It's liberating to call the beast by its true name: shamelessly exploiting others' weaknesses to turn them into an instrument for achieving your own aims.

I'm scared of losing

Anybody who plays the game of power and doesn't like losing has taken on an extra burden. Not only does he or she have to

---

*Baltasar Gracián, *The Art of Worldly Wisdom*, translated by M. Fischer, Barnes & Noble World Digital Library.

think about aims, strategy, moves, the arena, and their opponent's weaknesses, but they also have to consider the potentially damaging consequences of the game.

They will be taken captive by the horror of an unhappy ending. Any loss in income, status, or reputation will haunt them. And this in turn will mean that they'll be more concerned about controlling their fears than playing the game in its truest, most calculating form. What's more, most politicians are astute at sensing fear and will turn these weaknesses to their own advantage.

"Anybody who is scared of the consequences puts himself at a disadvantage." I remember learning this when I was young; I've never forgotten it. I first heard it from an older and wiser colleague. F—— and I were talking about a meeting I was due to have the next day with my director about a severance deal. We were still discussing terms; I had a lot to lose.

"Well, F——," I said, "just suppose that P—— refuses ..."
"Wrong," said F——. "You're allowing yourself to get sucked into negotiations. You're getting yourself worked up about the negative consequences and directing all your efforts at avoiding them. Let go. What can happen? You'll have to pay a forfeit on your leased car? The anticompetitive clause will be invoked? You'll have to leave behind everything you've built up? You'll have to start again with a bad taste in your mouth? Is that really so dreadful? Accept it, and you'll see how much stronger it will make you. What's more, I've known P—— for quite a few years. If he gets a whiff of your fears, he's bound to exploit them. Get rid of the fear. Let it go."

I was silent for a moment, letting the message sink in. He was right: if you're scared of losing, you've already lost.

I object to office politics. One has to be open and honest!
Many bosses, gurus, and other assorted windbags are scornful

about political maneuvering. If you listen to them carefully, you'll realize that what they are really concerned about is any negative consequences for the business.

So they'll say something like this. In a company where political games are played, people are always on their guard: in their offices, in meeting rooms, and during discussions. Everything they say or do is tainted by suspicion. Because of this, the windbags say, real issues that could provide essential information to management are never discussed. Everybody is on their guard, not wanting to say anything that could be used against them. Politicizing business erodes the very structure and foundation of individual relationships.

Others stress that all this political stuff detracts from the pleasure people take in their work and undermines their relationships with colleagues and bosses. The result—to use refined language for a moment—is that the motivation, inspiration, and energy to supply high-quality services and products disappear. Politics depresses turnover and saps the added value, the profits.

Still others stress that politics leads to division among the troops, so that individual units enter into open or guerrilla combat with one another. This paralyzes the flexibility that is so essential in business. Politics, according to this view, leads to disintegration and bankruptcy.

Nevertheless, we have to dismiss all these views as false. After all, organizations are a collection of individuals or groups of individuals who depend on one another in the pursuit of their own goals and interests. It's strange that this lesson—one that has been discussed exhaustively in manuals about organizational management—should be so easily forgotten once the first step is taken on the workplace dance floor.

It may be satisfying to explode the myths bandied about by

bosses, gurus, and other windbags, but it's far more interesting to ask why politics worries them so much. There will always be political machinations in a company, whether out in the open or buried underground; the only choice people have is whether to accept them gracefully or allow them to operate like a red rag to a bull.

The only explanation I can give for this touching and childish denial of the inherently political nature of organizations is a stubborn belief in a utopian world where blessed are those that labor, and brother does not turn against brother. We don't want it, so we deny it exists. In the past, the notion of utopia was a cancer that lodged itself in deliberations about society; today it has not only spread to the ideas of organizational experts and change engineers, but also infected the claptrap spouted by those who are supposed to be in charge of businesses: the bosses.

And this is where we find the divide that so many people have experienced: a painful attempt to straddle the gulf between everyday corporate reality with all its political machinations and the brave new world presented to us by well-meaning gurus.

I hate creating victims

Most people will tend to agree with this statement: yes, I really do hate creating victims. They'll also do everything they can to avoid confronting themselves in the cold, unfriendly morning light of a bathroom mirror: villain, villain, villain. And that's a pity, because a whole lot of people have no need to feel guilt; just a few minor regrets, perhaps.

Let me explain a little more. First we have to decide exactly who deserves the label "victim" and who doesn't. It goes without saying that people who experience the effects of avalanches, floods, volcanic eruptions, and extremes of cold and heat are victims. And the same is true of those who suffer the consequences when technical faults or human errors cause a factory, oil refinery or airplane to burn down, blow up, or crash.

And then there's a third category: people who, because of the deliberate decisions of others, see their ambitions, aims, interests, and sometimes even their lives come under threat. Are they victims? It depends.

In day-to-day conversation, we often talk about "innocent" victims. Anybody who is blown up by a suicide bomber, run down by a drunk driver, burned to a crisp because of some negligent coffee-shop owner, or robbed by a fellow citizen has every right to consider himself a victim, since he has never been party to the action nor even played in the perpetrator's arena.

If you are a victim, the label entitles you to sympathy and generosity from people around you. Benefit concerts, memorial parades, government support, and charity drives can all be organized for victims.

But should a company's bosses and employees hijack this label? Can they claim the benefits of victim aid? Have they been hit by natural disasters or technical malfunctions, or suffered from indiscriminate, indefensible acts of mindless violence?

No. Not at all. They aren't victims, but losers. Anybody who works enters the ring, the battlefield, the arena of their own free will, and therefore loses all claim to innocence. From that moment, you can win or lose. The battle is on. It's up to you to develop and follow your strategies in order to secure your victory. And if, in your desire to win, you have to hinder others, crush ambitions, shatter dreams, thwart plans, wreck careers, do away with people—that's the way it is.

In the battle within and between organizations, there is only one rule: eliminate the options for the other party, or at least restrict them, so that you emerge the winner. What it all boils down to is simple: your interests or mine. Every company is loyal to its own wallet; that's exactly the sort of loyalty every employee should have as well.

Why do so many people worry about creating victims? It's because they are suffering from "victimitis," a virulent disease that has spread through management and organizations and is assuming the scale of an epidemic. People suffer from it when they stand in the arena and are on the point of winning ... and then choke because they simply don't have a winner's mentality.

Instead, they stare into the wide, tearful eyes of the loser: the last and most deadly weapon, something that can destroy even the doughtiest fighter. It can turn him weak and defenseless in the blink of an eye, because it appeals to his compassion and generosity. He will no longer fight for his own interests, but champion those of the weakest.

Enough of this feebleness. If we in business scheme and plot and undermine others, then we mustn't indulge our Florence Nightingale compassion, but rather glory in the exhilaration of our imminent victory. Let us never again confuse victims and losers. Let us never again accuse ourselves of being weak or being a victim.

The end justifies the means

I don't know who has it easier: people who agree with this statement or those who disagree.

The former will have to live with the knowledge that if accepted means don't achieve the required effect, they must be prepared to reach for unaccepted—unacceptable?—means. The latter will have to live with the knowledge that their ethics prevent them doing anything more, and so condemn them to losing the fight.

I have more admiration for those men and women who use devious methods to look after their own interests than I do for those who allow themselves to be slaughtered because of some high-minded principle. The former accept responsibility and don't mind getting their hands dirty, however distasteful it may be. There are, of course, emotionally autistic executives who seem indifferent to the effect of their actions—the kind that refer to staff as "low-hanging fruit" to indicate how easily they can be removed—but the majority seem to know just how far they can go and where the boundary between acceptable and unacceptable behavior lies. That they nevertheless make tough, well-considered decisions imposed on them by circumstances and feel the bitter pain of regret demands our respect and admiration.

This is the opportunism preached by Machiavelli in *The Prince*: "And you have to understand this, that a prince, especially a new one, cannot observe all those things for which men are esteemed, being often forced, in order to maintain the state, to act contrary to fidelity, friendship, humanity, and religion. Therefore it is necessary for him to have a mind ready to turn itself accordingly as the winds and variations of fortune force it, yet, as I have said above, not to diverge from the good if he can avoid doing so, but, if compelled, then to know how to set about it."*

Anybody who has never got their hands dirty has never really lived.

So there we have it: thirteen statements that tell us something about the fascinating life of the rat in our organizations. You can now read the results of your audit, including a description of the three types of rat that I've identified. After that, I want to take you into the arena ...

---

*Niccolò Machiavelli, *The Prince*, New Albion Press e-book.

Scores

Up to 12 points: *Stupid rat.* You are so innocent. Charming. But the time will come when you'll have to shed your naiveté. You work is becoming increasingly complex. Don't resist the evil in this world; instead, turn it to your advantage.

13 to 20 points: *Clever rat.* You're not doing badly. You already possess quite a bit of verminicity, but it's not perfect by any means. You'll have to make quite a few more blunders before you master the discipline of the rat. Try putting yourself in the other person's position. You could profit from the experience.

21 or more points: *Filthy rat.* You are almost a true rat. You know about winning and losing. You understand the game. Either you are naturally talented, or you have already learned to crack the whip. Have you considered the drawbacks of being a rat? Lust for power, isolation, loss of integrity? Because otherwise you could become dangerous. Or go stark raving mad.

3 | **In the Arena**

In the first part of my letter I concentrated on the basic attributes of the rat. In the next section, I shall describe the bureaucratic tricks and moves you'll need in your work on politically complex projects.

First of all, we'll take a look at the arenas in which we compete. I'll offer you a few tools you can use to understand the arenas in your own environment. I can't stress enough that any political battle must start with lucid analysis, good interrogation, and excellent observation—in other words, gathering information about everything and everybody involved. You must constantly ask yourself whether you understand what's really going on, whether you understand the other party, and whether you understand yourself. Got it?

Am I in an arena?

The first question we must ask ourselves is whether our senses need to be sharpened, our muscles flexed, our adrenaline boosted. If, like the philosopher Nietzsche, you see something behind everything and suspect a power play in every action, this question is superfluous. You'll already be on your guard.

And yet—and yet ... there are degrees of machination. You'll have experienced periods at work when there is a certain peace, stability, and openness. You could of course maintain that even these periods are deliberately staged in order to achieve higher productivity—that they are some clever move by your boss or the shareholders to make you run faster. And yet—and yet ... as a rat, you'll look at such quiet periods in a different light to those of great turbulence.

But it doesn't really matter whether you think everything is all part of a power game, or whether you think some periods are less prey to political maneuverings; you'll still have to decide for yourself whether you are in an arena.

Arena indicators

There are a number of indicators that can help you decide whether you should be vigilant, in a state of alert, or actually bearing arms.

The checklist below may assist you. It contains a number of statements about the organization, the project you are working on, and your own attitudes. The more "yes" answers you give, the more likely it is that your present project is subject to considerable political machinations, and the more you should be on your guard.

	Yes	No
Ambiguous aims?		
Contradictory interests?		
Differences in values?		
Changes ahead?		
Unpredictable work?		
Ghosts from the past?		
Confidences?		
Rats on board?		
Am I open about what I'm doing?		
Do I have a bad feeling about what's going on?		

Let's look at each of these individually.

Ambiguous aims? In some companies, ambiguity seems to rule the roost. Amid trumpet fanfares, the big boss explains the mission and vision. But he can only do this by mouthing abstract twaddle. "We are number one in the field of interim management because we are results-oriented, creative, and think with our clients." This kind of spiel may sound wonderful, but when you want to make it concrete and specific, you have to ask: what is "results-oriented"? What is "creative"? And what is "thinking *with* our clients"? And you realize there are several possible interpretations.

Still, some companies have to deal with greater ambiguity than others, simply because some aims can be defined more concretely than others. Building a Web site in 200 hours to meet agreed specifications is much easier to define than "tailor-made home care." The more ambiguous the aims, the greater the freedom one has in interpreting them and the more vigilant you must be, because everybody interprets them in their own way.

Contradictory interests? Any project leader's handbook will stress that you have to be aware of all the interests and demands involved in your work.

Many professionals develop a nose for this. And yet I have seen top-level project managers bite the dust because they were convinced their proposal had the best content, and were astonished that other people thought differently. The proposal that includes the best aim may not be the best in human terms.

The most reliable rule of thumb is to assume that everybody initially promotes their own interests and only then looks at the bigger picture. Since the ability to analyze interests and desires is so crucial for the company politician, I have devoted a separate section to it later in this letter.

Differences in values? In some companies, you encounter factions with totally different values. One faction strives for peace, security, and continuity. Another wants nothing to do with this, checks the latest share prices once an hour, and aims to "make it" as quickly as possible. Yet another regards work as a means of personal improvement. And you can find other factions as well.

You can be fairly sure that these values reflect the desires of the people concerned, and that when push comes to shove, they will wish to realize these desires. Most employees and managers learn in time to repeat, parrot-fashion, the values that their company wishes to impose on them. But that doesn't mean they will abide by these values, except perhaps for one or two deluded individuals who have no personal desires and look to the company to supply them.

If the values of the various factions are highly disparate, this provides a breeding ground for political collusion.

Changes ahead? Nothing transforms a company into a boxing ring better than yet another change process. Every organizational change represents a shift in the power structure. It might be a merger, an expansion, new working methods, the introduction of new computers, new forms of education, new methods in nursing and care—but they all mean you'll have to do different things in a different context under different conditions. Change is all about shifts in the dependencies of people and groups: some get more power, others less.

It's wrong to assume that resistance to change is always irrational. Of course, many people experience change as threatening, and almost all of us have asked at some time whether we can do it. Whether we *want* to do it. This minimal irrationality can be seen as a fear of the future; with the necessary information and practice, it can be dispelled.

No—most resistance is extremely rational. Rational, that is, if you see it in the light of "what is good or bad for me." If you judge it irrational, you are making one of the biggest analytical mistakes you can make: treating people who are fully aware of their own aims as crazy and therefore suggesting they require therapeutic rather than political treatment. You've forgotten that change automatically implies a shift in power and that this makes it one of the arenas for the rat.

Unpredictable work? In some periods at work, you can predict fairly accurately what you have to do and how it will turn out. Organizations don't like chaos, and do everything they can to prevent unpredictability.

When you work in a company or department where things seldom stay the same and where you constantly have to seek out new partners, there's a greater chance you'll be confronted with politics. When work is predictable, the results are equally so. But things are seldom like this in most professions. Goals must be constantly redefined and new directions must be charted and followed.

Ghosts from the past? Dirty tricks are going to be played in any organization, and some people are better at them than others. You should assume there will always be somebody who wants to get their own back. A powerful businesswoman once told me: "These people have obstructed me at every turn and played some very dirty tricks. But I know that, and I will get my own back. Not immediately, because I'll have to wait for the right moment. I'll watch, observe, and then strike. In a month, a year, or even years to come." And this from a woman who kept firm control over her emotions and had an impressive record in social and emancipation issues.

If somebody like that allows herself to be swayed by resentment, how can people who are less talented at handling the rational and emotional fare any better? What would we do?

You have to be aware that in organizations, political struggle and verminicity frequently have their roots in long-ago events.

No harm can be done by undertaking some undercover delving into the past.

Confidences Whenever somebody in your company takes you into their confidence, or when you do the same and conversation turns to some juicy scrap of gossip or complaints about somebody else, then you know it's time to turn up the heat. Because it seems something is taking place that can't be talked about openly in the team or in general discussion. Complaints and gossip should alert you to the fact that something is going on.

I remember working for a bank as an external consultant. One of the employees took me into his confidence. I shouldn't be too ambitious, he warned. He'd been like that in the past, and hadn't been promoted since. I replied that the bank had become much more open and honest, and had assimilated these qualities into its culture. He looked at me with scorn.

Two weeks later, a manager was relieved of his position because during a departmental meeting he had been stupid enough to suggest a greater degree of self-management and employee participation in the development of business plans. Well, that wasn't the idea. Everything could be discussed, except the division of power. The case was exhaustively discussed around the coffee machine, in the corridors, by the copier, and in the cafeteria.

Furtively.

Rats on board? The last check we can do is to determine whether there are any rats among our colleagues: people who have a sharp nose for their own interests, a healthy admiration for their own ego and a talent for manipulation. As soon as they appear in our vicinity, we should rush to take cover behind a wall of paranoia: are we being screwed?

We know by now that a good rat is hard to spot, having all the outer characteristics of a normal ethical person. That inhibits a rapid unmasking. Yet there are a few simple rules you can follow to help you recognize a rat. Rats are notoriously vain. They crave recognition and acclaim for the superior tricks they have devised. They may not tell you about their current schemes—what coups they are planning, who they are trying to undermine, what act of revenge they are preparing—unless you are a member of their inner circle. On the other hand, they may well tell you about their past feats.

The art you must develop is to get them to talk about their careers as rats. Heap praise on them for their successes. And find out whether they were bold strategists or manipulators ...

Am I open about what I'm doing? The previous sections dealt with the organization and other people; now we must turn the spotlight on ourselves. You can use yourself as a good source of information. (I'm still assuming that you are neither crazy nor disturbed.)

Answer the following questions about the talks you have with your work colleagues, your superiors, and your employees:

- Do I tell them about the dirty tricks I've pulled?
- Do I tell them about my personal interests?
- Do I tell them what my reasons are?
- Do I tell them why I tell them in this way and not any other?

If you answer these questions with a "yes," then you have a

naive way of operating, a beguilingly carefree style.

That means one of three things: you are a naive rat—a stupid rat as described in the self-test—and you are simply open; or you are a superb rat and use your openness and honesty to disarm the opponent, which therefore makes you (bravo!) strategic; or you are a rat on standby and don't detect any verminicity around you, so why bother (again bravo!)?

Remember that if you don't tell others about everything you are doing, or if you adapt the truth somewhat, you have a perfectly good reason for it. Which is: you believe others will use the information to their own advantage and against you.

Do I have a bad feeling about what's going on? I'm a firm believer in intuition. Not that I see any hidden potential in it or consider it a divine talent. Alas, my take on the subject is rather more mundane. Intuition, to my mind, is nothing more than *tacit knowledge*.

In business life, we must take our suspicions, our irritations, our refusals, and our objections very seriously. They are triggers that will take us on an expedition to the source of discomfort. They are unspoken hypotheses about what's going on. They encourage us to put into words the information we have obtained through interrogation, spying, and reading, before testing them for truth or falsehood. Much of the rat's work is detection. If you think intuition is the last step in reaching a conclusion, you are seriously mistaken: intuition is the rat's first step.

Now you've checked out the ten indicators, you should be able to tell whether you need to wake the rat in yourself or not; whether you need to be vigilant or not. The more "yes" answers you gave, the more likely it is that you've entered an arena, or will enter one in the very near future.

Size of the arena

I must talk a little about the size of the arena. Who are the fighters, and whom can we ignore? To adopt the jargon of corporate life: who are the key players?

If you've been with a company for any length of time, you'll know the answer: the human resources manager is a player, and so too is the internal auditor; but the divisional manager isn't a player—at least, not in this particular contest. In refined language, we refer to these people as "the relevant actors."

There are certain situations where it is much more difficult to identify the principals: during a change process, in new projects, or during developments in and around the company. You'll have to set off in search of the key players. If you possess any journalistic urge to uncover the facts, it will prove an advantage.

You can map out the arena by:

- Getting people in your vicinity to climb on their soapbox
- Searching around for project plans, organizational charts, and other documents
- Asking your employer
- Keeping up with the gossip at the copier, coffee machine, and so on
- Building a relationship of trust with secretaries and general administrators, who often know more about the place where they work than they realize.

A sensible and classic approach is to reproduce all the information you've gathered in a graphic form. I like to use a whiteboard for this (a piece of paper does just as well), representing each player with a little circle. This force-field analysis—as it is sometimes called—gives enough room for indicating individual relationships. I've even met people who have a program for it on their laptop. That's taking things a bit too far, I feel, because the arenas are not places of monumental spectacle.

If, despite all your analytical efforts, your sleuthing, and your dedication to unearthing interrelationships and struggles, you still don't fully understand what's going on, then you may have restricted the area of the arena too much. There are probably other players in the game, at higher levels or in the background, whom you haven't yet identified.

Don't fall into the trap of doubting yourself and your capacities as a rat. You probably just have to dig deeper to discover the missing link. Arena analysis is archaeological work: you have to recreate complete pots from tiny fragments. So if you can't understand what's happening even though you've conducted a thorough investigation, you'll just have to search further.

The opposite mistake is to allow people into your arena who have no right to be there. Not everybody is equally important; not everybody is advantageous or disadvantageous to your interests and aims. You must eliminate these people from your thoughts, not only because they distort your picture but also—which is worse—because they demand energy from you that could be put to better use against your real opponents.

A novice in the rat game is more likely to include too many people in an analysis than too few.

Check people's interests

When you have inspected, both as spectator and participant, the gladiators, you would be wise to check their interests. The pitfall to avoid here is forgetting that you are an interested party yourself. You should undertake this exercise in order to ascertain whether other people's interests are in conflict with your own, or mutually compatible. Do you know, by the way, what your deepest desires are, what you are really after?

Although people's interests and desires are legion, a number found in companies need to be discussed further:

- Goals
- Cashing in
- Professional development
- Fun
- Status and prestige
- Security and safety
- Private life
- Power
- My enemy's enemy ...
- Love and hate.

Goals Everybody in a company must have something to show for their efforts. They must get results. Your goals are the things on which you are ultimately judged: they represent the expectations, whether explicit or tacit, that others—or yourself—have about your performance.

In many companies, these goals are explicitly spelled out: you have to achieve so much turnover, bill an agreed number of hours at a specified rate, care for a certain number of patients, fire 400 people. But goals can also be vague and implicit: you must get the department in shape, you must turn this cultural center into a successful and profitable business, you must come up with new ideas for mobile products and services.

Some people set goals for themselves: they want to start their own business, find a less stressful but more rewarding job, become financially independent. Everybody has some goal or other—for other people or for themselves. This latter, by the way, is often called "a wish list."

Cashing in During the last few years, particularly in the mad nineties, many professionals held the entrepreneur in high esteem. He was the superhero ready to take on the world, the Übermensch of the global economy. Many people dreamed of starting their own business and becoming financially independent. In the fast track of telecommunications and IT, these dreams were far from rare. That it would all end in tears was something nobody expected.

As I was preparing to write this letter, I had lunch with some people who had recently started a business and now employed 100 staff. They were proud they had built up the company from scratch in just four years. When I asked them what had prompted them to start their own business, they looked at each other and answered hesitantly, "Well—we wanted to build up a real company." I looked at them expectantly, showing them I thought there was more to the story. And then, as if they had been caught off guard, they added, "Well, actually we wanted to become financially independent within five years." So I said, "Oh, you mean you wanted to cash in by selling your company?" They gave an embarrassed nod of agreement.

Their real interest was in building up a business that they could sell for as much money as possible. They knew they could never get rich as professionals charging by the hour; for that, you have to go into trade.

Later, during lunch, they complained that it was incredibly difficult to motivate their staff and get them involved in the business. They couldn't understand it: the employees were given every opportunity for personal development, they had the challenge of becoming the market leader, and the staff outings were always fun. But the employees were right: why should they feel any commitment to a company that only existed to make its owners rich?

There are countless companies like this dating from the 1990s. Wonderful stories, a true mission, a nice in-house coffee shop, all concealing the deeper intention: the owners want to cash in.

Professional development People's interests have a lot to do with the stage in life they have reached. There are development aids on the market that show exactly what stages you have to go through, from helpless baby to acceptance of mortality. Such aids are useful in determining age-related interests.

Young professionals often say they want to experience everything in a whole range of different situations. They want to test themselves in order to discover what they want—and what they don't want. Their value is that they have too much energy and can work long hours. They are the draft horses in a company. Give them a new situation—they'll think of it as a challenge—and watch them gallop away.

Professionals in the *middle* period of their lives are often lost in a dense forest, just like Dante. They lose the plot and start thinking of bizarre plans like starting a surfing school, buying a farmhouse in the Dordogne, or following a career as an illusionist. They like discovering new interests, a new goal. In terms of interests, these "midlifers" are totally unpredictable: sometimes they are ferocious fighters, willing to risk everything; at other times they become listless, withdrawn, reluctant to take a single step. When forming coalitions, don't put too much faith in them; their unpredictability is dangerous.

And then there's the last group: managers and professionals who are nearing the end of their career and have three or four years left to go. They may have reached the zenith of their power, or perhaps have recently been deposed. As they often say themselves, their interests lie in rest and reflection. They prove something that has been believed for centuries: that an active life (*vita activa*) is always followed by a life of contemplation (*vita contemplativa*).

Such people are welcome guests for managers, business-people, and officials provided they have enjoyed a successful career and are pleasant to have around. They become a confidant with whom you can discuss important issues concerning the heart and the wallet. They pose no threat, since their career is coming to an end. Those professionals who have heard the approach of old age and successfully shifted their sights gain the most enjoyment from these last years of work. If you need a confidant, keep your eyes open for someone in their fifties. They have benefited from a good education, have often enjoyed a brilliant career, and know all the tricks of the trade, whether through observation or participation.

There's a world of difference between these brilliant elders and that other group of seniors, the cowards, who seem to suffer from life-induced constipation. These horned cattle know only one love, one idol, which they worship every minute of every day. Beware of them, because they have only one passion in their lives: their pension! And prepare yourself, for these people can be the worst rats of all.

Why? Because they are ruled by fear. They are terrified that they might not reach the end, that they might go under between now and that farewell dinner organized by the management. They do everything possible to defend their one interest. And because they no longer understand that there are a dozen different ways of doing something, they turn everything into a life-and-death struggle. They are ruthless warriors in a strangely moving all-or-nothing combat. We would find them endearing if they didn't pose such a threat to our interests. Arm yourself against these old-timers.

Fun Over the last few years, I've noticed that a lot of people are on the lookout for Fun. He is over 6' 2", midthirties, well dressed, thin, and extremely animated. Fashionable glasses complete the picture. Here we have an enthusiast who has learned all the right refined language from gurus at a whole range of seminars.

This is Fun: "No, I'm not worried about the money. Of course, I enjoy the odd luxury. But my core competence is my ability to enthuse people, get them on board, and then work together with them as a team. Develop all their talents. We have to make things enjoyable. It's all about *fun*. Let's have fun together." He waits for me to agree with everything he's said. But I can't, no matter how much I want to. I like him, but I freeze. This "funnification" of work simply doesn't do it for me. Perhaps I'm just too suspicious.

What constitutes "fun"? People who are looking for fun generally share three ideas. First, work has to feel like play. The division between work (where you have to sweat your guts out and just get on with it) and recreation (where you can relax and enjoy things) has to disappear. Second, working with others mustn't be too complicated. Difficult people and conflicts aren't part of the human condition, but rather aberrations that have to be cured as quickly as possible. And third, when the fun-seekers talk about fun, they really mean mobility and speed. Work has to move fast and be full of short, sharp adventures. You have to zap through it.

Funsters are simply unfocused avoiders, naive and credulous. But you'll see how easy it is to manipulate them, with fun mirrors and fun food!

Status and prestige In the political arena, you should never forget status and prestige. Deep down, everybody shares a need for recognition: "I am an autonomous woman. I am a great manager. I am wealthy. I love fun. I am a courageous and conscientious employee." Few people have so much autonomy or self-confidence that they don't need this recognition by others.

Most courses, training sessions, and seminars in personal growth and assertiveness fail. That means that in any power game, status and prestige always come into play. You'll come up against them time and again. What should you do if you injure the honor, the pride, the status of your opponent? There are two rules: one white, one black.

The first is that you do everything you can to prevent your rival losing face. Allow them a means of escape, even if every bone in your body protests. Be pleased with everything they do for you. Don't hurt them unnecessarily, certainly not in other people's presence. Avoid kicking them when they're down. They'll be eternally grateful, and think twice about paying you back for all the tricks you've played on them. There is no better breeding ground for revenge than wounded dignity and tarnished status.

If the white strategy doesn't work, you'll have to follow through with the black rule. It's hard. You have to disarm your opponent and render them harmless. You must destroy them totally, so that just like those politicians and managers who fall from favor because of a dubious expense account or a friendly bribe, they remain powerless for the rest of their lives.

You can make good use of people's need for status and prestige, because those who are susceptible need others to confer these things on them. If you can praise them in public, do so. Do they get a kick out of famous people? Introduce them to celebs. Do they need compliments? Heap them on. Do they require adoration? Then adore them!

But at the same time, give them lessons in the principle of tit for tat. Their dependency must ultimately serve your own needs.

Security and safety Many people are scared of working alone, of being isolated and lonely. They consider it vital to be included in a group or team. This makes it easier to understand their actions; they've decided they have less chance of surviving on their own than if they enjoy the protective shield of a team or department.

Good rats will manipulate these fears and insecurities. They create a permanent threat of exclusion and isolation as punishment for behavior that doesn't suit their needs. Giving somebody the silent treatment because they have acted against the interests of the company or consorted with the enemy is an example. Conversely, rats reward good behavior by drawing others more closely into the warm embrace of the group. This is a good way of disarming unwilling elements.

Private life Once upon a time, there was a businesswoman who made a fortune selling shares. When journalists asked her why, she replied that she was chiefly concerned with ensuring a safe life for her children and her children's children. She must have been riddled with fear and distrust of the world to have sought security through share deals. If there is something even more desirable than entrepreneurial success, it is not needing to rely on that entrepreneurial success any longer. Here was someone who defined her interests as her private life.

Many employees do the same as managers and directors: even though they bandy about refined language and say they are interested in the company, in their personal development or in some deeper good, they actually seek their interests in their private lives. This doesn't go much further than the desire for peace and quiet: a vacation chalet somewhere far away with a fence and a gate to seal it off from the outside world. In fact, most people think this way.

Power I once had a conversation with a successful interim manager of a bank in Rotterdam. He told me all about his career. His story started with his first project, in which he had to manage not only himself but also a colleague. Although he found this difficult and demanding, he nevertheless succeeded. He achieved his aims on time, within budget, and to specification. A class act, you would have thought.

He followed this with a second project, in which he was required to manage two people ... Well, you've guessed it: each successive project required him to manage twice as many people as the one before. They multiplied like the grains of wheat on the chessboard in the parable of the king and his subject.* He finished up with 800 employees and two management layers to manage them.

Some people judge their success by the power they acquire. For them, power is an urge, just like sex: it rears its head from time to time but can be only briefly satisfied, and never completely fulfilled. Only by declaring a firm "no" to this lust for power—just as one sometimes has to say "enough is enough" to sex—can one bear the constant feeling of unfulfilled desire and overcome the emptiness.

---

*Wanting to reward the subject for his loyalty, the king agreed to grant him one wish. So the subject asked the king to place one grain of wheat on the first square of the chessboard, two on the next, four on the next, and so on, doubling the number of grains each time until the board was full. Being lousy, at math, the king agreed, not realizing that the amount of grain on the chessboard when it had been filled in this exponential way would be greater than all the grain in the kingdom, and all the grain in the world.

In your arena analysis, try to decide which men and women are striving for more authority, regardless of the content over which they preside: the job-hunters, the professional board members, the chair-hopping notables, the vainglorious, the sperm-spillers. Find out who has never learned to utter that liberating phrase: enough is enough.

My enemy's enemy ... Earlier on, I showed you how to recognize when you enter an arena. I then discussed the extent of the opposition and the interests you are likely to encounter. There's one rule you must never forget: calculate how the interests of others promote or obstruct your own interests, or coexist indifferently with them. That's the first thing you must do in your arena analysis.

But there's another aspect to discuss, and that is how to interpret the various interdependent relationships. Or as Gracián says, my enemy's enemy is my best friend. Amid the mists of conspiracy, we must always learn who loves whom, who hates whom, and why.

Love and hate ... in a movie theater Let's take a look at love and hate in the form of a case study, so that we can fully appreciate their intricate workings. Let's go to some provincial town, somewhere out in the sticks, where the political and cultural elite are engaged in a life-and-death struggle about a movie theater. The main characters are the director of the theater, the councilman responsible for culture, the mayor, and the director of the town's concert hall.

The movie theater, previously a merchant's office, has been carefully restored and stands proudly above a block of beautiful row houses dating back to a time when people had an eye for such things. It's a normal town that you might find anywhere.

Nothing in the surroundings betrays the *petite histoire* that is brewing here.

The movie theater moved to this location two years ago after extensive renovation. The idea is that it should pay its own way and generate income by offering a full range of events: movies, concerts, exhibitions, corporate events, and so on. Because there is a swelling current of cultural entrepreneurialism, the movie theater hasn't been absorbed into yet another department of the cultural bureaucracy, but has been set up as an independent foundation.

The director, who got the job because of her commercial and organizational acumen, adopts a policy of prudence and fiscal frugality and manages to stay within budget for the first two years. Quite a feat, but one that is negated by a whole lot of investments that the movie theater is compelled to make: the roof leaks, the heating doesn't work properly, the kitchens are inadequate. As a result, the books are showing a hefty deficit.

Nevertheless, the mayor considers the movie theater one of the jewels in his crown. He visits it every week with some delegation or other, often from far-flung places. The director wants to make a name for her theater; the mayor wants to make a name for his little town.

The mayor is also a fervent supporter of the controversial concept of culture as business. Despite belonging to the same political party, the councilman for culture holds a different view: he believes that local government should have a big say in cultural matters, because if everything is left to commercial interests, all you'll have on offer is either elite art or mass entertainment.

The advent of the movie theater is a thorn in the side of the director of the concert hall, but for different reasons. He is already responsible for the historical museum, the music school, the fringe theater, and the old church used for receptions and big concerts. He has set himself up as the process manager of the town's cultural activities: "I want all cultural activities to be in tune with each other." He has been able to do this because he was previously second-in-command at the department of culture.

A lot of gossip within the town's bureaucratic community is directed at this director's passion for empire building, especially among the local government officials who have had personal experience of the man's determination. The movie theater is the town's only independent cultural body, something that was decided by the town council.

Because of the movie theater's deficit, concern is mounting that it will be declared bankrupt and its director dismissed. The director thinks she has performed well: the deficit has arisen only because she had to make unforeseen provisions for the leaky roof, the faulty central heating, and the cramped kitchens. If the council had overseen the renovation properly and given her a usable building, nothing would have gone wrong.

The other three actors see the situation as an opportunity they can turn to their advantage. The mayor still believes in cultural entrepreneurialism, and doesn't want to lose face. In addition, he is almost as pragmatic and commercially minded as the director of the movie theater. They understand each other.

The councilman for culture smells his chance. A mistake made in the past—creating an institution independent of the council—can be repaired.

And the director of the concert hall has recently invited the director of the movie theater for a little chat, where he proposed a new management model in which all cultural institutions would fall under one body so that the assortment of activities could be fine-tuned. He would then become general manager, while the director of the movie theater, thanks to her proven organizational ability, would be appointed manager of facilitating services. She would be in charge of buildings, managers, and administrators, and report directly to him.

The director of the movie theater rejected the offer. She had been warned by a local government mole that the director of the concert hall was on the rampage ...

We'll stop the case here, although its history would paint a sobering picture of how things are organized in bureaucratic circles. Let's take a closer look at the various relationships.

That's something the director of the movie theater has done very well. She had to determine who were her friends and who were her enemies. In fact, there were two axes in this arena: the axis formed by the director of the movie theater and the mayor, and the axis formed by the director of the concert hall and the councilman for culture.

The bureaucratic machine resided largely in the former camp. The mayor was the most important ally of the director of the movie theater. Their interests ran parallel in two important areas: both were firm believers in independent cultural entrepreneurialism, and both took a pragmatic approach to solving problems.

As far as the director of the movie theater was concerned, the director of the concert hall and the councilman were her greatest enemies. Both considered her a thorn in their side. The movie theater was an aberration that should never have been allowed to see the light of day—an independent foundation, indeed! They would do everything in their power to destroy it. They loved each other. The councilman saw the director of the concert hall as somebody who could realize his deepest ambition: to return all aspects of culture once again to the council's fold.

And the director of the concert hall did his utmost to feed that dream: he would help the councilman on the condition that he was made the director of all cultural institutions. That was the deal they had agreed.

And the officials in the town hall? They were the eyes and ears of the director of the movie theater, her best friends. They were the enemies of the director of the concert hall and the councilman. They wanted nothing better than to frustrate their plans, get in their way, and eventually bring about their downfall. Then the just order of things would be restored, and past injustices would be revenged.

I can reveal that in the exhilarating battle that ensued, the concert hall director and the councilman were toppled from their thrones. The movie theater foundation remained independent. What happened? Well, perhaps I'll tell you all about it some other time.

With this everyday story of love and hate in a provincial town, we leave the arena. In the next section of my letter, I want to tell you about the sources of power that we have at our disposal. Or not …

4 | **The Sources of Power**

When you enter the arena as a rat, you have to determine which sources of power your enemies can tap, and which you can draw on yourself. This knowledge is vital because it will help you decide whether you can attack immediately or whether you first need to marshal additional sources of power.

Your sources are necessary for success, but certainly not sufficient for victory. Even when you are holding all the trumps, it's the way you play the rat game that ultimately reveals your mastery. You can make a stupid mistake, or a rival can preempt you. And you also need a large dose of luck. Sometimes losing is nothing more than bad luck.

We list here nine sources of power for a rat:

- The strength of the monopoly
- The breath of the structure
- Power to facilitate
- Technology
- Formalities
- The body as weapon
- "Big Brother" repression
- Networking
- Sorcery.

In the following paragraphs, we'll look at each of these in more detail.

The strength of the monopoly
In every company there is somebody who has power because of something they possess that is both scarce and in demand. Fortunately, these people aren't always aware that they

command a monopoly position and own a weapon they can use to manipulate us for their own ends. A monopoly is excellent for us, because we can exploit it to make and keep people dependent on us. But we have to be extremely frugal in the way we use it.

In our economy, businesspeople, professionals, and technicians profess gladly to embrace free-market competition. Let's face it: it's all a sham. Given half a chance, any business would become a monopolist like a shot so that it could set the rules in its own interests. Consider the major software corporations. What's good for them is good for you.

You have to seek out that much-desired object, service or knowledge that is available only to a very few. But where do you find it?

Backup sources Most organizations have people who can make your life easier or harder. They get things printed, arrange for your computer to be installed, get you a cellphone, prepare a room for your meeting, and help you make that new DVD player perform its tricks. They represent sources that could be helpful to you.

This will, of course, make you feel dependent on them, and you'll have to use all your psychological skills to get them in the right mood to help you. Fortunately, most of these people will have done customer-oriented training sessions that are intended to teach them servility and thus prevent them becoming arrogant monopolists.

But everybody knows that technician or secretary or department that is going all out for a monopoly position. Rather than allowing ourselves to be irritated by such people, we should learn to admire them for their determination to seize power.

If you are able to acquire such a source of power yourself, consider yourself extremely fortunate. One down!

Knowledge, expertise, and experience An extension of such backup sources is your own knowledge, expertise, and experience. These too are sources of power. Unfortunately, knowledge and know-how have become commodities that are easily acquired, and your lead over others is based on nothing more than the fact that you have been working longer and have gained more experience.

Today, you are constantly being encouraged by all and sundry to share your knowledge, because that benefits the company. Be very careful: sharing your knowledge means sharing your power source. And the more people you share it with, the faster it will be exhausted.

You'll notice that as time goes by, many professionals specialize in certain tricks. Recognized for the talent that they are and applauded by all, they become the undisputed master of a certain problem area or competence cluster. They acquire power.

Make sure you have some knowledge and experience, no matter how small. You may be able to use it to get people under your thumb.

Security The fiercest demon for many organizations is the demon of uncertainty: you don't know whether the enterprise you are running together will ever prove successful.

Companies have introduced a whole raft of measures designed to eliminate such uncertainty—or, as it is usually put, to prevent the boss being confronted with surprises. Monthly reports, market research, trend analyses, bribes, cartels, quality management, education and training, and planning can all be seen as expressions of uncertainty. "Will it be all right? Are we still in with a chance?" Let's face it, all these business "sciences" are nothing more than present-day versions of examining entrails, studying star charts, and reading tea leaves or tarot cards.

Management gurus, HRM prophets, and organizational experts earn a very good living by such means. With their elegant Gucci bags filled with checklists, applications, and presentations, they've become professional uncertainty-busters. They have you in their power because your uncertainty has driven you into their arms. If somebody else hadn't beaten them to it, it's likely that one of them would have stood up and proclaimed: "I am the way, the truth, and the life."

So if you are able, with words and deeds, with smoke and mirrors, to make other people think you can save them from their uncertainty, they will be eternally grateful: you will have become the light in their darkness.

But if, on the other hand, you can accept your own uncertainty in the same way you might accept a headache or a sore knee—these things happen; you can only do your best; sometimes you're lucky, sometimes you're not; you have good days and a lot of bad ones—then you will suffer less from fantasies about unhappy endings and not be so keen to seek the help of professional uncertainty-busters. They won't have any hold over you. Of all the sources of power, this one is the easiest to disable.

The breath of the structure

Employees work. Bosses make sure of that. And the bosses' bosses? Are they concerned about the work process? Well, I'm sorry to tell you this, but the answer is no. What they are concerned with is the organization and its permanent rebuilding (otherwise known as organizational change).

They get things moving—or not.

You can feel the breath of the organization. Here's the power of the structure. There's the board where the generals move their armies with long sticks. Look at the company as a study in logistics. And see the shifting around of bodies and goods.

Inclusion or exclusion You can give or deny power to your employees by the place you allocate them in your company's logistics structure.

It's a matter of analysis and calculation. And it was taught me by the director of a nursing home in an affluent district, who explained in great detail how he got recalcitrant nursing staff back in line. What was going on? Well, the director had been involved for some time with an important change that would give nurses a different set of responsibilities. The plan was to change from task nursing to team nursing.

An aside for all those who aren't actively involved in health care: task nursing means that the nursing function is broken down into individual tasks (washing buttocks, taking temperatures, chatting, putting in false teeth), and that a different nurse will visit each bed for each task or cluster of tasks. At busy times of the day—in the morning, say—you might have a whole succession of nurses visiting your bed: assembly-line nursing, in other words.

Now you can imagine that nobody—patient or nurse—really likes this. It robs patients of their humanity, treating them as little more than objects that have to undergo a number of processes as efficiently as possible. Team nursing offers a less mechanistic alternative: a small group of nurses undertake all the nursing requirements for a small group of patients. Patients see the same few faces, and mutual respect can be developed.

When the director explained all this to me, I could do little more than answer, "That's what everybody wants." To my amazement, he said: "No, not everybody. I have a group of nurses who want to continue doing things the old way. They don't want this change." Of course, I wanted to know how he was going to handle the problem and what he intended doing with this stubborn group.

When I asked him, his eyes glimmered. He pointed through the window to an extension to the main building. "See that wing there? I've opened a new department on the top floor for psychiatric patients. Eventually it will become a closed department. All the patients are severely demented. And I'll put all the nurses who don't want to work in a team in there too. They can carry on nursing in their old way. The old people won't mind; they won't even notice ..." He paused, and leaned forward. "And I won't notice those nurses, either."

When I drove home, I couldn't help being impressed with all this, not least with the opportunism and calculation. In later years, I would encounter more examples of how to use this source of power; for the moment, though, I was just a young consultant.

Some problems can best be solved by locking them up somewhere; by making use of the organization.

Power to facilitate

In an earlier part of my letter, I told you about the concert hall director who was in charge of his town's cultural institutions. We should keep our eyes peeled for this man, because he embodies a source of power that's becoming increasingly prevalent in corporate life: the power to facilitate. It's a source you can quickly make your own as long as you know how to get along with people.

This is the way it works. In many companies, a lot of

changes are taking place: new methods, new technologies, new markets, new bosses. Sooner or later, some of these changes and improvements become embedded in projects. In these—as we all know only too well—people work toward achieving a specific goal within a predetermined timescale with the use of certain resources.

But there are other developments in an organization that are far more open-ended and less regimented. In these, attention is directed not so much at an aim but rather at a process: the flow of changes that must ultimately result in renewal, in the emergence of something new. For our concert hall director, it was a move toward a bigger and more varied cultural program in the town.

The point is that in such circumstances you have to deal with a range of parties, all with their own interests and aims. You can't simply silence them, get them disqualified, or hinder them in some other way, because they too have their sources of power. In this sort of situation, somebody is often appointed to follow the process and, where necessary, to persuade people to give ground a little, break down a dam, or help with the sandbags. Their role is to make things easier: to facilitate.

These process assistants derive their power from the process itself, and can play an important (and sometimes even impartial) role in it. You can draw up agendas, flatter people, threaten them. You can be as sweet as honey or as sharp as vinegar. You can use the whole repertoire of intrigue once you've been appointed master of ceremonies.

Technology

I can't stress enough that technology is itself a source of power. The range and nature of its accessories, instruments, and techniques determine the interaction of power around the machines themselves: what they do and what they control.

The huge technological changes in the world of banking provide a good illustration. In the old days, you used to have to visit some building to arrange your financial affairs; nowadays, you are encouraged to do everything with telebanking and get your money from an ATM. The new information and communication technologies have virtually eliminated the need for physical premises.

This means that fewer employees are needed in local branches, and those left are less important to the bank. Conversely, the power of those who create and control the technological infrastructure has greatly increased. As branches disappear, so too does the personal contact between the bank and its customers. So it's hardly surprising that experts in the field of customer relationship management (CRM) are becoming more important. Their job is to consider the possibilities offered by impersonal systems for what they like to call the "personal assistance" of clients.

The introduction of new technology shifts the balance of power. Some groups of employees will have to surrender some of their power, and you can expect them to resist; it makes perfect sense from their viewpoint. Others will gain more power.

Formalities

An important source of power can be found in all sorts of rules, regulations, procedures, statutes, and laws. We call these formal sources. You can find tips about how to uphold your rights and how to evade your responsibilities. All we need to do as a rat is to live by the rules—or by the spirit of the rules when that suits us.

I was once taken into the confidence of a building contractor who had joined his wife's family business. One gray morning, drinking coffee by the gallon, he told me his story. I'll repeat it here because it is such an excellent example of how to make use of formal sources.

When the contractor joined the company, its shares were in the hands of his wife and her brother: half each. His brother-in-law had indicated that he wanted to leave the company and would sell his shares for a reasonable price. One day, sitting at the kitchen table, they agreed that the brother-in-law would sell his 50% of the shares to his sister and her husband over the next five years. Then he would be able to enjoy a well-earned retirement.

But what happened? Well, two years later, having sold 20% of the original shares to his sister and her husband in the meantime, the brother-in-law changed his mind and decided to hold on to the remaining 30%. He decided he was much too young to retire. And as so often happens in family businesses, nothing about the share transfer had ever been consigned to paper.

To make matters worse, the brother-in-law started blocking much-needed improvements to the company. Whenever a decision had to be taken, he stood in the way. Wielding all the power that his 30% stake conferred on him, he became adept at obstructing plans for the company. Its statutes stipulated that important decisions had to be backed by 75% of the shares; the contractor and his wife owned just 70%.

They were in a jam. And that wasn't all. The brother-in-law, who was also one of the directors, did less and less, and simply didn't have the ability to run the company. He was preoccupied with riotous living and easy money.

The contractor wanted to boot his brother-in-law out of the business as quickly as possible and get his hands on the remaining shares so that he and his wife could take full control. A business consultant friend came to their aid.

First, they started compiling a dossier on the brother-in-law. Their aim was to prove to a judge that he had repeatedly made mistakes. He'd been given every opportunity to find his feet and work constructively; in the end it was his own fault that he had to leave. And at the same time, the conspirators prepared to play another formal card.

We must pause here to give some background. Like many family businesses, this one had a complicated structure, with a series of companies that were owned by other companies within the group. This labyrinth was controlled by a foundation with an administrative office where decisions about directors were taken. The foundation played a crucial role in the ensuing battle because its board took decisions on the basis of one person, one vote, regardless of the number of shares any member held.

Everything boiled down to counting heads and scrutinizing the statutes. The board of the foundation had four seats, held by my confidant, his wife, his brother-in-law, and their mother. Mother refused to be involved. She didn't want to side with either of her children against the other.

The statutes also threw up a bulwark against the kind of attempted coup that so frequently afflicts companies. The relevant clause stated that whenever there was a proposal to change the board, all board members must be present at the board meeting, and at least three of them must vote for it. This made it impossible to fire the brother-in-law from the board, since one person would always oppose the proposal (the brother-in-law), and one would abstain (Mom).

Fortunately, my confidant and his wife found a loophole in the statutes. If the full board *wasn't* present at a meeting, those members who did attend could call a new meeting that would have to take place within eight weeks. At the subsequent meeting, a simple majority of votes would be sufficient to carry a motion. And if there was no majority, then the decision would be taken by the board member with the greatest number of votes —in this case, my confidant's wife.

The plan was put into action. A board meeting was called with the dismissal of the brother-in-law as one of the items on the agenda. The contractor and his wife knew full well that Mom wouldn't dare take sides, and probably wouldn't turn up. They were right.

The second meeting never took place. The brother-in-law knew he would lose no matter what he did. The case had been prepared; the board of the foundation would fire him, and he'd probably lose in court as well. A week after the first meeting, the contractor warned his brother-in-law that he would continue to press for his dismissal. Not only that, but if he were dismissed, the foundation's board would propose a motion that no further dividends be paid out on the shares he still owned.

Ouch! The brother-in-law would be holding shares worth hundreds of thousands, but earn nothing on them at all. Unless ... unless, of course, he sold the remaining shares to his brother-in-law over the next three years for a reasonable sum, and was prepared to accept a reasonable severance offer. That's exactly what he did.

And the family? They're still at war as we speak.

The reason I've given such a detailed account of this case is that it illustrates so perfectly the use that can be made of formalities. And believe me, such formalities are used day in, day out in fights like this. In a town just like yours.

Always study the rules, the procedures, the statutes. Knowing the formalities may prove of inestimable value to you.

The body as weapon

The body, that bag of bones and warm water, shouldn't be neglected as a source of power just because it is, with all its peculiarities, right at hand.

Power Although I don't suggest in this letter that you use force to solve problems, I still have to point the possibility out to you. In some situations, the power struggle in and between companies is accompanied by well-aimed blows.

Not so long ago, a feud broke out between several taxi companies. They tried to make each other's lives as difficult as possible, sometimes by using the body as a weapon of power. Quite a few taxi drivers sported black eyes. Everyone thought they had good reason and allowed their emotions to take over. But they were only human; they were only defending their right to make an honest living.

Even in classical times, a distinction was made between battles of words and battles of blows. The first were part of governance; the second, of war. Young men were trained in both, but the two were treated quite separately. Under no circumstances should they ever be allowed to mingle, for fear that the whole political culture would collapse.

The same must hold true for rats: the mascot for amoral professionals who pursue their own interests at all costs. Don't allow the two areas to merge. And remember that the body offers more than mere strength and violence.

Gender One of the nicest ways of manipulating people is to take advantage of their gender. Some professionals can easily be exploited through their masculinity or femininity, no matter how much they would like it to be otherwise.

There are forces at work that are more dominant than the

conscious mind, and manipulating them can bring you enormous satisfaction because of the remarkable results you can achieve. Take care not to reject stereotypes and prejudices according to the current moral climate; you must judge them by their usefulness to your schemes, not by whether they violate the unique intrinsic worth of a human being. Let's look at a couple of examples to see how you can make use of stereotypes.

I was once the confidant of a manager at a technical university somewhere in Holland. She was the living embodiment of people's worst prejudices about women in high places. In our discussions, she wasn't just businesslike; she was cold, arrogant, contemptuous, distant, and made you feel that everything was all your fault. All that was missing was a wart sprouting hairs on her chin. She was a superbitch on a seven-series broomstick. Yet even she had a feminine stereotype buried deep within.

I remember the time I made a complaint. I said that a few directors were blocking all sorts of developments; it was impossible to do business with them, and they were really annoying. Perhaps I hit on the right words, or tone, or body language; whatever it was, I've never witnessed such a rapid transformation in my life. In the blink of an eye, this witch turned into a mother. Her sharp body become softer, rounder; her hooked nose straightened before my eyes; her breasts swelled with milk; and maternal hormones started pumping through her veins.

"That's disgraceful. I'll make a note and investigate. I won't have it. This shouldn't happen to you." I'd made my point, and she swung straight into action.

From that moment onward, I realized that this calculating monster had a weak spot: her maternal instinct. I only had to play the young boy to manipulate her in any way I pleased, like a movie director with an actress.

If you think only women can be manipulated in this way and men are above such things, I'll have to disabuse you. Men are just as predictable. The only thing you have to know about men is that they prefer to face danger head-on so they can enjoy the adrenaline rush. Then they'll swing into action for you.

Let me illustrate this with a domestic example. Imagine you have a man at home who doesn't listen to you. All you want him to do is drill a hole in the wall and hang up a painting. Of course, you're quite capable of doing it yourself, but you'd rather not.

Experience has shown that simply asking a man to do something doesn't often produce any noticeable exertion. So if asking doesn't help, then what? The only thing that will help is to send your man out to war so that he can return a conquering hero. And why begrudge him the pleasure if it furthers your aims?

And so, one Sunday afternoon when your man is in the living room, you rummage around in the attic and come down with the electric drill and all its accessories. You spread everything out on the floor in front of you (and your man) and start picking up one thing after another. Finally you choose the wrong bit for the wrong hole. And then just watch how quickly he swings into action. He recognizes the danger—you are going to drill a hole! —gets his adrenaline fix, and wants to make things safe. "Here, let me do that."

Now pay attention: you must *not* say yes at this point. Instead, turn up the threat even more, so that the adrenaline gets a chance to circulate properly. "Are you sure, dear? You look so comfy there on the sofa ..." And that's it: he surrenders, a victim of his own manhood. All you've done is pressed the right buttons: threat and challenge. Just a few seconds later he's drilling the hole in the wall and you're standing next to him with the vacuum cleaner, sucking up the dust.

Do these mechanisms work every time? Can you *always* manipulate women through their maternal instincts and men through their pugnacity? Of course you can't; real people are much more complex. But don't let that stop you exploiting gender stereotypes if the opportunity presents itself.

Age Sometimes an aside in a book or a conversation sticks in your mind more than the main topic. It's as if you suspect a deeper truth lies behind the words, an experience full of wisdom, or a sense of hope. It's no coincidence that many philosophers have written aphorisms; still, that's beside the point.

When I was a student in my twenties, my tutor—a large man with friendly eyes, a thick mane of gray hair, and a luxuriant mustache—confided that in the various boards of which he was a member, he was required to do less and less work. I looked at him expectantly. "It's true. I don't have to justify the things I say as much as I used to. I can't do anything about it. It's all to do with my age." These days, younger colleagues tell me that I have things a lot easier than they do because of *my* age.

I certainly don't intend going down the well-worn path that says young professionals enjoy the fruits of their impetuous and relentless energy while their elders must depend on maturity, experience, and gray hair. Such a sweeping analysis does a disservice to a more subtle and complex reality.

But I do want to encourage you to view your age as a source of power, and to exploit it by accentuating or concealing it as circumstances dictate. One caveat, though: a junior who acts much older than their years or a senior faking youth are equally suspect to most people.

I once gave a lecture to students on a course that was very much geared up to the practicalities of business life. I was surrounded by young men and women clad in pinstriped gray and navy suits. They had clearly learned how to imitate the ways of their seniors, yet they all came across as fake because they were trying so hard to conceal the very thing that should have been the source of their power: their youth.

On the other hand, I have also watched a colleague do a presentation where he used the language of energy, decisiveness, "let's all join hands and make a go of it," while his eyes—yes, it was his eyes—sang a different song, of peace and gradual retirement. When I talked to him afterward, he confirmed my suspicions.

Numbers Of all the sources of power, unification is one of the most common: strength in numbers. It appears in many guises: trade unions, clubs, political parties, environmental organizations. Its might lies in the number of members it can muster.

Rats will, in all their machinations, always be on the lookout for allies who can help them advance their aims. Anybody who uses such terms as "consensus of opinion," "platform," or "presenting a united front" is trying to increase his power by multiplying the number of allies he has.

"Big Brother" repression
The better you understand your opponent, the better your chances of eliminating him or getting him to work for you. It's no coincidence that many handbooks dealing with the power game pay considerable attention to methods of controlling people through close surveillance. We can distinguish three aspects.

Spying The true rat will pose as friend yet operate as spy, Gracián once said, summing up the first aspect of panoptic repression.

Much of your work as rat consists of "human intelligence"—the field in which secret services specialize. Like them, we rats in the organization must infiltrate groups that could be important to us so that we can spy on managers, colleagues, customers, and suppliers and dig up dirt about them. Do you have a list of suspects?

The driving thrust is to collect information about hidden intentions, strategies, plans, and activities so that we don't encounter surprises in the game and can take evasive action in advance. To do this, we'll need to track down the appropriate reports, infiltrate top managers' courts, and regularly interrogate people in our artless and innocent manner. Don't forget that the organization is full of people who, because of jealousy or revenge, are eager to leak information to us.

The secret is to pose as a friend. We must make people think we can be trusted and have only their best interests at heart; we must act as professional coaches and radiate the conviction that their cares, worries, ambitions, and dreams are safe with us. Pose as friend, act as spy.

Go undercover. Don't stand out; be absolutely sure your opponent doesn't fathom your soul, your weak spots, your interests, or your aims. But don't become an enigma either. Don't give suspicion a chance.

Measuring If you are in a position to measure people, consider yourself extremely fortunate. You are holding a weapon with which you can inflict considerable discomfort on a lot of people. By using all sorts of measuring techniques, you can render a whole range of things completely transparent: performance, ambition, personality type, profitability, competence or incompetence, hours worked, hours present, Internet use, telephone use .... It's entirely up to you.

Every organization wants insight into the behavior of its employees. But what is so strange is that the more independence you have in defining your aims and your working methods, the more rigidly you are measured and monitored. The absence of a supervisory manager or foreman doesn't imply that your organization's desire to know everything there is to know about you has in any way diminished. It's rather that in the interests of efficiency, other methods of observation have been chosen.

Nothing instills greater fear in an organization than people doing their own thing. And if you work for a company that preaches initiative and self-government, look out for the control posts. You'll generally discover them in the measuring systems your company employs. Don't be deceived: even if you work for one of these fashionable self-governing companies, you will still be monitored. You may come and go as you please, but you'll always remain visible to others so that they can intervene whenever necessary.

This aspect of measuring has two consequences for you.

On the one hand, you must ensure that you become as invisible to the company as possible—unless, of course, high visibility suits your plans. Keep your work and your private life separate; don't let on how you really feel about things; don't chat about your deepest desires. Find out where all those measurements have to be reported; keep a private email address; take out a private cellphone subscription. Be careful about coaches, and don't tell your colleagues and managers too much. Cherish any small hiding place where you can keep out of the sweeping spotlight.

On the other hand, you must sharpen your talent for

measuring and exposing others. Use checklists. Get your colleagues to take personality tests. Measure your employees to the point where they are about to erupt in fury. Use your measure to find a treasure ...

Self-correction The advantage of visibility is twofold. First, panoptic power leads to self-correction; second, should this prove inadequate, it leads to corrective measures. For most people, it's enough to know they are visible. Then they will act properly. In addition, observation brings you a deeper understanding of your opponents' strengths and weaknesses.

And there is an even greater advantage. Many will look into the face of measurements and draw their own conclusions about what they can and can't do. They will immediately grasp whether their natural place is with the breed of born leaders, or whether, because of some minor genetic fault, that path has been closed to them. You won't even have to hold one of those "bad news" discussions.

Measuring exposes the finest examples of the professional breed. You can make your selection and breed further. Lesser examples can be consigned to another office far away or eliminated altogether through corporate euthanasia: dismissal.

Networking

Knowing the right people in the right place at the right moment; a datebook filled with telephone numbers; here lies the source of considerable power, as I have already written.

Remarkably, there are still many professionals who are so busy with their work that they neglect the most important thing: their network. Their priorities are all wrong. You need a network for information, clients, piggyback rides, assassins, allies, money and ... power. Set aside three days a month for your network, and you'll enjoy the sweetest fruits.

Types of network There are so many networks you can use. Within your company, you should locate the court network because, as we have already seen, it is a valuable source of information. Then there is often a network of middle management: men and women who regularly meet in some consultation group or other. The advantage of this management layer is that they can make or break a proposal from top management, or at the very least severely delay its implementation. And don't forget to mine your network of professional colleagues. They can help you realize any ideas you may have.

Perhaps the networks outside the walls of your company will be more important: the government officials at municipal, state, or federal level whom you will need on your side. Or do you need the assistance and support of an employers' organization or trade union? Or can you expect more of an ethnic network, a women's network, or something similar? What about business networks, like those claques of businesspeople and directors who constantly pass the ball to each other?

You'll discover that some networks are as impenetrable as the Mafia, excluding anybody who isn't a member of the family. Most, however, have an open character.

Junctions I'd like to draw your attention to something I call junctions. Most networks overlap each other. You can develop power by identifying and occupying the junction between two networks. That way, you can act as an intermediary between them.

From time to time, every network will need information from another network. By occupying the junction, you'll make both networks dependent on you for information. You patrol the borders and let through only that information that is relevant to them—and you.

Sorcery

The Nazis are often credited with being the first group to use modern communication techniques to manipulate the hearts and minds of the masses. It's easy to see where this idea came from; just look at the photographs of lights, fires, flags, and stadiums packed with thousands of people. And yes, the Nazis did make use of rhetoric, thunderous words, bewitching images, the power of symbolism: sorcery, in short. Power that was created by manipulating symbols, icons, and drama. These things appealed to people, and still do.

Today, this source of power has become even more refined through the choice of words, logos, clothing, and perfume. I will give you two contemporary examples.

Architecture Somewhere in a town near you is an organization concerned with creativity and knowledge. Not a particularly large company, but one that has achieved a high profile because its director is a great networker.

Its office is located in a stately boulevard, lined with equally stately mansions. And if you were to ask whether there are old trees too, I would have to say yes. You enter the office through a narrow hall, and suddenly find yourself in surroundings that are light years away from the glass palaces that line the expressways. Warm colors, a banana palm, paintings, a spiral staircase to the bar in the basement, and a multitude of mirrors. A large, high-ceilinged room—perhaps an elegant salon or reception hall in a former life—overlooks an area, carefully divided up by glass panels, that features plants, chaises longues (or should I call them daybeds?), wooden floors, and, on some high wooden platform, the latest flat-screen computer monitors.

It's a casual, warm, inviting area that bears little resemblance to the usual professional cubbyholes. You are bewitched by the architecture, both outside and in. The icons of modernity—glass and steel, transparency, business—no longer hold sway, usurped by the romantic revival: organic forms, emotion, creativity.

The way your company is "dressed" evokes a subtle mood that permeates the business. Whether your building is strictly functional or aesthetically pleasing, it conveys a certain lifestyle and dictates attitudes, emotions, and a style of working.

Spectacle You can also soften people's hearts and minds—and thus manipulate them in the direction of your choosing—by using spectacle. Perhaps you'd like to create a greater feeling of solidarity, or bring out the vital qualities in your people, or just entertain them.

I was once the guest of a department that was deep in the doldrums. It had suffered internal conflicts, people had left, and the market was depressed too. People needed to close ranks. And so a few highly talented men and women organized a wonderful spectacle that left nothing to chance and used every element of symbolic manipulation to the full: location, music, food, play. The guest speaker, a happiness guru, had obviously taken instruction from a drama teacher and knew exactly how to play an audience. Within five minutes, everybody was eating out of his hand. His session was about creation and wish fulfillment and things like that.

But, you may ask, what was so clever about such a clichéd approach to pampering the personnel? Well, everything was exaggerated; every element had a cynical tone. Any possibility of resistance by the personnel was translated into some part of the day. Cynicism was used to expose cynicism. No escape was possible. Indeed, such is the nature of high-quality spectacle: it allows no escape. Individual resistance, individual questioning, is short-circuited. The mind is prepared to receive the New Insight.

Don't be shy of using art, mass media, rhetoric, or anything else that culture has given us to manipulate people's emotions, desires, and dreams. Great leaders set themselves apart from others by their ability to direct people's dreams and desires, and redefine their reality, so that their lives once again have meaning. We might also call this gift, this source of power, emotional management.

Nine sources of power—monopoly, structure, facilitation, technology, formalities, bodies, "Big Brother" repression, networking, and sorcery—that everybody has at their disposal. Nine sources of power to enrich yourself and impoverish others. Nine sources of power to use opportunistically.

5 | **Tricks and Ruses**

In the past few years, newspapers have been full of stories about devious bosses, corrupt officials, and builders on the make. Without knowing about their underlying motives and interests, we find it hard to fathom their tricks and ruses. But let us zoom in on their methods. How do these rats go about their business? What is their favorite type of work? In what can they be our example?

I've heard a whole lot of stories about rats and the way they operate over the years, both at first and second hand. Having analyzed these activities, I've used the results to produce the table below.

OTHERS	VIA A THIRD PARTY	MYSELF
• Bribery	• Choosing fronts	• Truthful lies
• Cutting off the retreat	• Gathering evidence	• Reputation management
• Exploiting weaknesses	• Victimization	• Being unpredictable
• Humiliation	• Leaks and gossip	• Wiping out tracks
• Undermining bosses	• Lobbying	• Knowing yourself

Repertoire of tricks

First of all, there are the activities directed specifically at others: your boss, your colleague, a national committee, the board, an interest group, a fellow councilman. With these activities, you are constantly screwing or milking the other person, or exploiting them for your own ends. Second, there are tricks that require a third party. Good rats have their marionettes and their courtiers. And third are the moves you can make on your own behalf. They revolve around what you say, what your reputation is, and how predictable you are.

We'll now go through the basic repertoire of rat tricks and ruses.

Screwing the other

Bribery There are always people around you who'll claim they are incorruptible and can't be bought by attention or gifts. Fortunately, reality tells us otherwise. At all levels of business and society, you can get people so worked up that they will roll over for you.

It's all about finding the right way of praising, tempting, rewarding, or punishing. Whether you're dealing with the most highly trained urologist or the lowliest clerk in the bookkeeper's office around the corner, trinkets, baubles, mirrors, a bottle of wine, a trip abroad will all help to bind people to you. If somebody receives a present, they'll want to do something for you in return—not because they want to please you but rather to soothe their own conscience. Profit from this human mechanism.

When you offer bribes, you must stick by four rules.

First, find a present that is proportionate to the scale of the service your minion is going to deliver. A bottle of wine to help you win a construction contract worth five million euros is a bit on the mean side. It's hardly calculated to make that government official writhe in ecstasy. You'll have to do better than that. Experience suggests that a couple of trips to some far-off country with the whole family will be much more to their liking.

Don't forget that bribery isn't particularly appreciated in Western society. Some companies lay down strict rules about it. You may have to devise some excuse for the person you are bribing, certainly if an ostentatious gift is involved. In many countries, doctors are given luxury vacations or pleasant bicycle tours. It's essential to assuage any guilt or rebellion they may feel. You can do so by ensuring that such events take place in an acceptable setting. So you dress up that ski vacation as a seminar, and that wine-tasting session (with of course that tempting little case for everybody to take home at the end) as a workshop to promote an informal exchange of ideas.

If you bribe a lot, you'll have to give your activities a veneer of respectability. Do what a lot of companies do: bury your bribing in departments with innocent-sounding names such as public relations, external relations, and training. This doesn't of course mean that these departments are nothing more than cover-ups; they do other things as well. But that doesn't really concern you. What matters is that you find a place for the bribes that suits you and gives you the best return.

And finally, some advanced lessons in bribery. Start small. Buy officials, contractors, and directors little by little. A small gift at Christmas is a good way to start. From then on, make the presents bigger and more extravagant until you reach a point where they forget themselves and sell their souls. Then they become dependent on you, because they can be blackmailed. Once you've reached this point as a rat, life becomes a ball.

Always know *why* you are paying a bribe: for that building permit you might not otherwise be granted, for a blind eye to those pesky safety regulations, or for that juicy computer order.

Cutting off the retreat A technique you must acquire is the ability to block your adversary's retreat. It's highly entertaining to limit someone else's options in this way. Do it well, and you'll be admired and feared. I'll give you an example that a colleague of mine tells. It is, perhaps, a better illustration of "crafty" than of "fraudulent."

It goes like this. He was a project manager for a major multinational, and was responsible for a worldwide change process. Standard machinery was to be introduced throughout the company. He noticed that one of the directors on the steering committee—the group that brought together all the regional managers and some top technicians—would nod "yes" in meetings, then say "no" when he got back home. This is, of course, a familiar and easy-to-recognize feature of all change programs: people who seem to be in agreement but then surreptitiously reach for every means at their disposal to frustrate and sabotage the process.

My colleague was seriously fed up with this director, who threatened to delay and perhaps even wreck the effort. To protect his own interests, my colleague had to come up with some sort of trick, so he decided to cut off his opponent's retreat. It called for a fair bit of preparation. He had to involve his opponent's boss in the plot too, but that wasn't too difficult, since he was a strong supporter of the renewal process. The only other things to arrange were a banner, some baseball caps, and a photographer.

After opening the next steering committee meeting, my colleague played his trump card. "I propose we devote an article to the new machinery in the in-house newsletter. My idea is to hold interviews with two people: one pro the change, the other anti. Personnel are asking for suggestions for the interviewees. What do you think?"

Most of the directors had a hunch that this had been scripted in advance, so they agreed—the director's boss most vociferously of all. They began calling out the name of the director who had been sabotaging things for the past three months. And so he was chosen, together with another director who would put the opposite point of view.

At that moment, the photographer came in on cue, brandishing the biggest telephoto lens anybody had ever seen. "Right, gentlemen," he said, "shall we get this over with? Let's go outside and take the photo. Do you have the baseball caps and the banner?" He spoke with absolute innocence, not having been included in the plot.

The project manager handed each director a baseball cap bearing the single word: "For." The banner was unfurled; it read: "We're all backing it." Everyone laughed, and started calling out the names of colleagues who should carry the banner. Led by the photographer, they all trooped out to the steps by the main entrance. On the left, the banner was held aloft by the greatest opponent of the change process; on the right, by its most enthusiastic supporter.

Two weeks later, an article appeared in the company newsletter. It said that the whole steering committee was fully behind the introduction of the new machinery, and everyone was determined to make the project a success. The dissenting director caused no further problems for the project manager or the steering committee. His retreat had been cut off. My colleague told me that this director actually appreciated the plot against him, and in retrospect thought it a highly successful coup.

And of course my colleague had had a ball. "When the photographer came in, I knew my plan was going to work. It was a wonderful moment. I relived it again and again all weekend." I can understand that. Getting the better of somebody in a friendly way; isn't that verminicity at its most elevated?

The technique, though, is still that of a rat. You maneuver your adversary into a situation where they have to choose the lesser of two evils: join in (which they don't want to do), or lose face and be exposed as someone who says one thing in public and another in private, and has no balls (which they don't want to do either). For the director, the less painful option was to give up and join in.

In advanced verminicity, you must always try to reduce your adversary's options to two evils, and ensure that the lesser evil matches your own interests. Some people aren't open to reason and can be won over only through pain. Those who won't listen find out the hard way.

Exploiting weaknesses For simplicity's sake, let's define "weaknesses" as those characteristics that cause people to give themselves over to others; in other words, those areas in which somebody is vulnerable. There's absolutely nothing wrong in revealing our weaknesses to our friends, confidants, or shrink, because they won't misuse the information. At most, they might be a bit uneasy about it.

In our working life, though, there are other forces at play. It's here that we fight for money, power, recognition, fame. We must be constantly aware that if others get a hint of our weakness and can make use of it, they will. And there we are with our repertoire of temper, inflexibility, fear, and vanity: a whole orchestra of characteristics from which to make a symphony.

Let our first tactic be this: never ever show the slightest weakness. That won't be easy, because almost every professional development process will encourage you—urge you, even—to confess all your traps, obstacles, sensitivities, and blocks. Don't do it! Keep your distance and play the game of "what if."

We must, on the other hand, be ever vigilant for others' weaknesses. We must plot their psychograms so that we can quickly learn which buttons to push, which valves to open, in order to get others to sing the tune we want to hear.

Of all these weaknesses, I want to discuss fear. Herein lies your most powerful weapon, one you can use to manipulate others. Fear arising from a real or imagined threat often lies at the root of people's behavior. Should we run away or turn around and confront the predator that is threatening us? Should we attack?

At work, there are three main fears, and we can understand them best if we follow the philosopher Hannah Arendt and make a distinction between "labor," "work," and "action."*

Labor consists of all the efforts we make to stay alive and ensure our body doesn't succumb to illness and decay. The implicit threat here is degradation, deterioration in quality of life, and ultimately loss of life itself. Let us call this the fear of ruin. Look at all those faces in front of you. They are managers who are scared of losing their jobs, of losing their certainties, because they are terrified they will be reduced to poverty, that state in which the vast majority of the world's population is forced to exist.

Work is the creation of an object: a product, a service, an organization. Unlike labor, which has to continue indefinitely, work can be completed. The threat connected with work is that it will fail, that it won't garner the prizes it deserves, that it might go wrong. Look at all those managers and employees agonizing, trying to control everything, and worrying themselves sick—all because of their fear of failure.

And finally there is *action*: making yourself known in word and deed to others, and belonging to a community in which you can have your say, think and contribute, and manage. The biggest threat here is that you are excluded, that you don't belong to the group or the network, that you become an outcast. We call this fear of exclusion.

---

*Hannah Arendt, *The Human Condition*, University of Chicago Press, 1958. I don't do her work justice with my analysis of fear; I am simply using her definition as a starting point in discussing how to prevent fear in companies.

No matter which aspect of your work you take, there will always be a fear—or a mixture of fears—involved: fear of ruin, failure, or underestimation. How can you exploit these fears? And are there people who are immune to them?

To start with that last question: yes, there are people who are difficult to manipulate through fear. One of their characteristics is that they have already anticipated any negative consequences that their actions may produce. They have either taken compensatory measures (lining up a golden handshake should things go terribly wrong, or exploiting an excellent network of contacts to help them find a new position) or else accepted the possible consequences as part of the game, so reducing the threat. Such stoical and calculating people do exist, but fortunately they aren't in the majority.

Now back to the first question: how do you manipulate fears? Easily. The recipe is simplicity itself. And once you know it, you'll recognize it in every walk of life: in the way married couples behave, in TV ads, in politicians' and managers' rhetoric, and in the activities of companies and organizations. Here goes:

Rule 1: Feed the fear of the other person.

Rule 2: Reduce the fear of the other person.

You first have to feed the fear of your adversary, magnifying that uneasy feeling evoked by being threatened. How? By confirming the image they have of their situation in an understanding and sympathetic way, and slightly exaggerating it. Imagine you know a project leader who suffers from fear of failure. You could say something like this: "Yes, it's very tricky. I respect your courage. A lot could go wrong. Would that have any consequences for you personally?" Nothing feeds one's fear better than the dreams, the images, the visions, the thoughts one already has.

An important movement in cognitive psychology is rational-emotive therapy (RET). This states that many of our feelings and actions depend on our thought processes. Therapists from this school teach you to replace inadequate thoughts or mental images with more realistic images. Say you are plagued by thoughts of disaster that make you feel angry or anxious; the therapy will teach you to replace these thoughts with more positive and dispassionate ones, such as: it won't be a disaster if my project fails; it will simply prove unfortunate for those involved.

What I'm trying to teach you here, though, is RET in reverse. You have to replace the other person's sober, fear-free images with strong, frightening images. A talented rat will feed the fears in word and image. Then you can make the other person dependent on you for their salvation, just as all the great gurus do. "Hey—if you were to do this or that for me, you'd see how much progress you'd make."

Most management methodologies—whether they are rooted in science or couched in more esoteric terms—are based on this one principle: they reduce your fear by offering you a way out. Why shouldn't you make use of this as well? Why not adopt these guru techniques yourself? What's stopping you? From today onward, use a few simple tricks to make other people dependent on you. And then exploit them.

What are the principles I am explaining in this letter? Well?

Nobody will ever accuse me of not abiding by my own rules!

Humiliation Anybody who knows history, or present-day society for that matter, is certain to have come across highly refined and opportunistic incidents of deliberate humiliation: the brutal belittling of somebody else simply for our pleasure, or to boost our self-confidence, or to get information that we want from them, or for some other reason. Generally we prefer to keep humiliation firmly outside our company's gates, or, if that doesn't work, at least out of our terribly correct thought processes. For if there's one thing we want to maintain above all else, it's the illusion of our good manners. What a pity!

We can make excellent use of the tactic of humiliation in our working life. Let me offer two examples to inspire you.

The first example takes place in a big company that needs to dismiss a lot of employees for economic reasons. It can happen; that's life. But it's difficult, all the same. The company wants to get things over with as quickly as possible, so it decides to send a letter to some employees informing them that they are dispensable. Others get a letter saying the opposite.

This humiliation is ingenious. To tell people there is no longer any work for them is one thing; to inform them that they are dispensable is quite another. It's a way of hurting people, of damaging their pride. It's telling people that they are superfluous and won't be missed. It injects a new emotional tone into the relationship: you don't matter to me. It implies that the other person doesn't really exist; it's like mashing tomatoes to pulp.

That people did take this tactic as a humiliation is evident from the number of rapid departures. The tactic proved extremely successful—a little too successful, in fact, because too many people decided: if they don't really want me here, I might as well leave. This example shows how damaging somebody's pride can help a company achieve its aims. Whoever thought it up must have a master's degree in verminicity.

The second example takes place in a run-of-the-mill company, and was related to me by the manager himself. He'd worked for the company all his life, both at home and abroad. Toward the end of his career, he made a mistake. He allowed himself to be hired by the international board of management to investigate a domestic department suspected of fraudulent activities, and to get things back on track.

But then the board of management was brought down, and with it my friend. Two days after the coup, the director of the department suspected of fraud called my friend into his office and told him he was being dismissed for economic reasons. The director was able to do this because my friend was officially employed as a consultant.

As you might expect, my friend started a legal process and claimed substantial damages. His opponent put pressure on one of his old colleagues to make false statements about his dysfunctionality—statements that were easily refuted. The denouement was fascinating. Just before the judge was about to hand down his verdict—and everybody was convinced he would award millions in damages—the company did an about-face and withdrew its dismissal. A very clever move.

The manager was told to report the next day to the head of Personnel & Organization—somebody who was very well versed in the art of employee humiliation. She arrived far too late, there was no desk available for my friend, and he had no access to the Internet. He had to fend for himself. The P&O bitch told him that in future he would be reporting to ... the manager who had made the false statements.

To make a long story short, a whole arsenal of organizational mechanisms was deployed to break my friend so that he would decide to leave the company of his own accord. That's what he finally did. He applied to a magistrate for termination of his employment and demanded damages, which were duly awarded. As you've no doubt guessed, the amount he received was much smaller than his earlier claim. But don't shed any tears for him. Rats don't do that. The company simply played the game well. Congratulations.

We can draw our own conclusions. If you want to get rid of people, humiliate and offend them; damage their self-respect until they leave of their own free will. It's much cheaper than a court case. And if you are a manager and have a personnel department, let them do the dirty work for you. Grant them the pleasure of acting as corporate executioner.

Just one more example in the same vein, this time about a math teacher in a high school. The poor man is burned out and can no longer summon the enthusiasm to teach kids the fundamentals of mathematics. All he manages to do is keep getting into conflict with them. The principal who told me this story has tried everything: personal talks, coaching, severance pay .... Nothing helped. The man doesn't want to leave, and it would be almost impossible to fire him. He's fixated on reaching retirement age.

"What could I do?" The principal feigned despair, his eyes gleaming with intelligence. "Well?" I replied. "The only solution is to get the man to go on sick leave before the summer vacation. For a long time. With all sorts of physical and mental problems. So that he becomes permanently disabled. And that's what I'm going to do. I'm going to break him. Humiliate him. Give him all the nasty jobs. Draw up a grueling timetable for him. Have him report to me daily. I'm going to destroy him mentally. He has to go. And if it has to be this way, then so be it."

For some reason, I support the principal's decision, but it's still the work of a rat. Humiliate and offend in order to achieve your personal aims.

Undermining bosses Of all the rat tricks we discuss here, none is more effective than undermining the boss. Anybody who has thought about this technique or experienced it will reach the same conclusion: you undermine your boss by making sure they don't reach their targets.

I've noticed that the people I talk to in large companies, even the trainees, are able to tell me within a few seconds how this is best achieved: "Simple—you make sure that they are held to account by their boss. You make sure they have to tell their boss that turnover hasn't reached its target or that the renewal process hasn't worked."

In order to undermine a boss, you must first know what they will be held accountable for by their boss; what explicit and implicit task they have been given. And, as a manager of a large European company recently added: "It's also handy to know what *their* boss will be held accountable for. Because then you will know what interests are at stake, and what can lead to your boss being fired."

Next, you'll have to discover what sources of power there are in your work and the organization. Means that will help you sabotage, divide, and sow confusion.

A senior manager in a Dutch company once told me about the time she had a director parachuted in above her from the UK front office. After a brief honeymoon, it became increasingly obvious that this man was totally unsuited to the company's culture. It was as though he was deliberately looking for mistakes he could make in order to create as much annoyance as possible. The senior manager decided with her colleagues to get rid of this man within a few months and have him replaced with somebody from their own ranks—namely herself.

The approach they chose was to maim the man and sap his power so that he wouldn't be able to achieve his goal: raising turnover by a certain percentage while at the same time reducing costs. First of all, they exploited the language difference. They resorted to linguistic misunderstandings in meetings, appointments, and reports.

Next, they adopted the "say yes, do no" tactic. Not that they said "no" openly; instead, they would talk about the Dutch culture and how it was vital to create a broad consensus. What they would normally have avoided like the plague, they now welcomed as a weapon: sweet-talking. Any idea, any decision, was discussed with as many people as possible, however remote their involvement. This, as you'll appreciate, caused endless delay.

At the same time, informal discussions were used to sow doubt about the director's competence. Middle managers, key employees, and opinion leaders were poisoned against him. The management team manipulated every bureaucratic and organizational means at its disposal to get its way. In the corridors of the UK front office, rumors were spread that things were going badly in the Dutch office. After all, it would be the front office that would make the final decision about the director. It was here too that ideas were spread about how the Dutch would handle the problem themselves, and who might be the director's most suitable replacement.

Step by step, the management team moved closer to its objective: the downfall of the Englishman. All its actions were carefully orchestrated. It's a mistake to think such actions arise spontaneously and from the heart. "That was certainly not the case," the senior manager told me.

You'll want to know whether the plan succeeded. It did. All the opposition prevented the director from reaching his targets, and he had to withdraw. She got his job.

So the rule is that if you want to get rid of your boss, you have to make sure they don't reach their targets. To that end, you can exploit everything within the organization that makes managing it so difficult. You create misunderstanding (by taking advantage of long lines of communication); you delay the implementation of a decision (by making as many objections to it as possible); you demotivate people (by manipulating opinion leaders); you adopt the role of victim so that you are not available (you report in sick at every opportunity); you create bad feeling about the management (by gossiping a lot and being constantly outraged); you frustrate the timely workings of company processes by starting too late, too promptly, incorrectly, or not at all (because there is little or no control).

Just imagine for a moment that you work in a transportation company; let's say a railroad company somewhere in Europe. You want to get rid of the management. Now you know what you have to do. Make sure they can't achieve their volume target: the number of trains that arrive on time. You may well achieve the same results as all those people who work for the railroad company ...

Fighting through somebody else

In this section, I want to take a look at those tactics that owe their success to their indirectness: those where you get somebody else to do your dirty work. In the previous section we saw that when you devise a whole campaign to undermine a boss, gossip and innuendo can magnify the effect. We'll look at a few examples of similar indirect techniques.

Choosing fronts One of the oldest rules in corporate politics (and in other areas too) is that you have to consider your front carefully and position it to your best advantage. It must be as far from you as possible. Let others bite the dust first!

I was once involved in a serious case of what's known in consultancy circles as "insulitis": an island culture within an organization. Departments hated each other; every gate was barricaded; the smoke of "we are the civilized ones, they are the barbarians" hung heavily over the battlefield. In that realm of tribes and warlords, in that corporate Gaza Strip, we consultants, like some UN representative, had to reintroduce civilization—or at least negotiate a ceasefire.

We chose the well-worn tactic of introducing a common goal: a new knowledge system for all combatants, organized by floor. Using a lobby system, we selected a few people from every department except the very worst. We chose the nicest, most approachable people we could find, and managed to persuade them to work on developing this new system. The department we excluded showed the greatest self-satisfaction and arrogance; that was the territory of the scum.

The group we had formed met to discuss things from their own personal perspectives; they weren't there because they were involved in managing the rest of the employees. Had that been the case, delays and undermining tactics would have been rampant. We didn't want any consultations.

In other words, we created a new player in the field and let representatives from the warring factions work together. And finally they came up with the idea—with a little encouragement from us—that their colleagues in the excluded department didn't know enough about the new developments. They freely decided—with a little encouragement from us—to enter into negotiations with these colleagues. And that was exactly what we intended. They had to go and fight with their own people. The front had to be moved right into the difficult department itself, and not be somewhere between the departments and us. From the very start, our plan was to sow disunity.

By deliberately not inviting the most hostile opponent, we had made a paradoxical intervention: trying to achieve something by doing the opposite. Had we attempted to bring the stubborn outsiders into line with the rest of the company, they would have revolted. By excluding them, we hoped they would feel so ignored that they would direct their anger at the exclusion itself. The angrier they got, the better we would like it. "What's all this about? Why haven't we been consulted? Don't we have any say in how things are run around here?" Our calculation proved correct.

The rule is that sometimes you can best ambush people by first keeping them out. But the key in such guerrilla warfare is to make sure you create the front that puts you in least danger.

Gathering evidence At certain times in your rat games, you'll have to look for your trump cards. If you don't have any right now, you'll have to acquire them. There will always be a moment of truth when everybody has to lay their cards on the table ...

I'll give you two examples. One concerns a former bureaucrat with environmental convictions who was able to delay many large-scale construction projects (new roads, housing developments, and the like). The other concerns a TV director who knew all the ins and outs about firing people, both as perpetrator and victim.

The art of gathering evidence lies in searching for material that can cast something or someone in a bad light. The ecological bureaucrat was a past master at this.

He had discovered that many reports on the environmental effects of construction projects contain faulty calculations. "I'd sit in my office for half an hour with my pocket calculator and check the tables. I made sure I discovered a number of howling errors, and I kept them on file. I knew I would need them later in any attempt to delay the decision-making process." I'll tell you exactly how he played his trumps a little later.

The TV director in my second example had to cope with a lot of dismissals. Cases of involuntary dismissal that come before a tribunal naturally take on an adversarial quality that's inherent in the work of lawyers battling with each other.

In this case, each party was busy building up its own dossier. The employer gathered incriminating statements and disappointing results. But the director was extremely ingenious in acquiring his trump cards.

He would regularly send letters to management asking them to clarify their decisions. He knew they weren't quick to respond, so he would send reminders. All these documents went into his file. Every letter that went unanswered was a trump card.

So you don't have to wait to get trump cards. You can also lay traps in the hope that the other side won't react, or reacts inappropriately. As long as you put everything down in writing, nothing can go wrong, and you can happily gather evidence against your opponent.

Victimization A real rat will always bear in mind the possibility that things might go wrong, and think about how to avoid unpleasant situations.

One much-used method is to allow a colleague to take the blame. Or, as Gracián put it some four hundred years ago: "Know how to let the blame slip upon another: to carry a shield against malevolence, is the wise strategy of those who govern, a thing not born of weakness, as the envious think, but of greater strength, to have on hand someone to shoulder the blame for failure, or to take on the punishment of general abuse: not everything can come off well; nor everybody be satisfied, wherefore provide yourself with someone to atone for your errors, and be a well for tears; even though it cost you some of your pride."*

Nicely put. We need somebody to make into a victim when our battles, our activities, our projects threaten to go wrong; that way we can stay out of the line of fire. When we look for scapegoats, the simplest solution is to pick a weak employee from whom we expect little or no resistance.

Imagine you are a project manager and your project seems doomed to fail on all fronts: you've missed your delivery deadline, you've gone way over budget, and the product doesn't even do what it's supposed to do. Business as usual. How can you make sure somebody else gets the blame instead of you?

Simple: you determine which group or part of the process is most critical to the product. That's where people should point the finger first. You appoint somebody who's not too bright, but very likable. You fill him with enthusiasm: it's a challenge, fascinating, you're really ready for this ... Then it's just a matter of waiting until the project goes completely off the rails.

The best moment, your finest hour, is when you have your employee report back on progress. Tell him how disappointed you are, and explain you have to be rigorous and remove him from the project. Two birds with one stone: you've misdirected your mismanagement onto the shoulders of this poor scapegoat and you've enhanced your own reputation through your decisive action.

The key to this technique is to spot somebody near you whom you can sacrifice. Be careful not to pick intelligent and forceful colleagues. They'll see through your scheme and do everything they can to hinder it by returning the bomb to the place where you least want it: your feet.

---

*Baltasar Gracián, *The Art of Worldly Wisdom*, translated by M. Fischer, Barnes & Noble World Digital Library.

Leaks and gossip Sometimes you'll need to leak information or spread ideas that damage somebody else's reputation. Either way, you must stay in the background and let rumors, whispers, and back-room gossip do their work.

A leak tends to be aimed at a particular decision-making moment; gossip has a more insidious character. Leaks call for timing; character assassination needs to be kept up constantly.

Let's go back to that ecological bureaucrat who was so good at sums. He'd developed an acute sense of timing for leaks. He knew exactly when a plan would be presented.

Just imagine: a group of builders, engineers, and bureaucrats have spent an enormous amount of time working on a new construction project. They have done endless calculations about almost everything because they know full well that some citizens and environmental groups will object. They finally dare to present their plans to the press and public at a happy little party. The PR company has set up a colorful tent for the occasion. Everybody polishes up their smile.

And there you are: a bureaucrat with ecological sympathies. So what do you do? You have a number of foolish mathematical errors filed away, and you realize the time is ripe to use them. A couple of days before the party, you call a friend at the local newspaper, explain your findings, make sure you remain anonymous, and then leave all the work up to them. Next morning, the day before the party, the flawed calculations will be front-page news.

More than once, this bureaucrat has actually managed to get parties canceled and create enormous delays while all the calculations were redone. By using the press, he has played his trump card much more effectively than if he had simply pointed out the errors in some back-room committee. Leaks can prove potent.

Now to gossip. Unlike leaks, which can be used in isolation, gossip and character assassination are supplementary tactics. You'll normally have to use them in conjunction with other ruses to get rid of an opponent. As the case of the undermined boss illustrated, there are three golden rules of opportunistic gossip.

First, use gossip to attack your enemy's credibility and rob their voice of authority. You'll need to be clear about which people your gossip campaign is targeted at.

Second, make sure you can't be identified as the source. Here lies danger. If you're found out, it will be your turn to have your character assassinated; your opponents will do everything in their power to tear your reputation to shreds. The art of gossip is to make sure it comes from different places. You'll need to whisper into the ears of several colleagues strategically placed throughout the company so that the rumor seems to emanate from all directions, just as a normal rumor does. This is where your network comes in handy.

And third, it's best to let rumors hitch a ride on a normal conversation. Halfway through your chat, casually bring up the subject that was your reason for starting the conversation. Mention that you are worried about somebody, are concerned about the way they are working, or simply don't understand how something could be happening. By adopting this cloak of innocence and integrity, you ensure that no suspicion can be directed at you.

Sowing dissent, suspicion, and distrust should be invisible to others, but perfectly clear to you.

Lobbying Of all the techniques I've listed, the most accepted and widespread is influencing others by creating and using a lobby. Anybody who isn't proficient at lobbying will achieve little in organizations and networks, even if they use regular channels.

Needless to say, anybody who aspires to the higher levels of the rat race won't get far without lobbying. Lobbying is based on the power of your network. The benefits of lobbying are widely understood not just in government and political circles, but also in the business world.

The principles are simple. Know exactly what you want, make a list of everybody you approach, and be clear about your objective in every conversation you initiate.

In Holland, one CEO influenced his company's decision-making process by lobbying his colleagues. Anecdotes have it that his board meetings were always very short and highly efficient. He would have admitted that all the important work was done in conversations outside the meetings.

Another example comes from a museum that was trying to get its subsidy raised. A group of professionals and volunteers gathered to conspire. They listed the most important influencers (bureaucrats) and decision makers (councilmen, aldermen, mayor) on a whiteboard, and then discussed who among the conspirators had the best access to these individuals and how much influence they could bring to bear. A former alderman who now did volunteer work visited the current alderman; a former judge took coffee with the mayor; and volunteers who belonged to a political party paid a visit to councilmen affiliated with that party. The subsidy was duly approved, although it was not as high as people would have liked ...

Lobbying pays; calculated, orchestrated lobbying pays even better. And if somebody with innocent blue eyes unexpectedly greets you with a friendly smile and starts asking for something in a roundabout way halfway through your conversation, beware: you are being lobbied. Don't shut the door on them; instead, think what you can ask them. They have revealed their dependency; now's your chance to use the lobby against them.

Yourself as instrument

In the rat game, there are a lot of things you can do for yourself because they involve you and no one else.

Truthful lies A good rat is an artist with words, using them to turn the most dismal failure into the most resounding success. You may regularly find yourself in situations where you have to explain events, plans, and deliberations. Some people will ask you to do so directly. Others, more intelligent, will choose a circuitous route to make you say what you'd have preferred to leave unsaid.

In this office guerrilla war, the more you're in control of what you say or don't say, the better. Think carefully before confiding in others. Secrets seldom remain secrets for any length of time.

The art is not to lie outright, but rather to use as many words as you can to say as little as possible about what you're up to. As a true rat, a seasoned manager, director, and politician, you'll no doubt have noticed a few tricks. Here are some for use in emergencies:

- Change the subject when things get difficult. Latch on to some adjective or relative clause and start philosophizing about it.
- Pretend to be dumber than you are. Apologize for not knowing anything about the subject in question. It's a useful tactic for gaining time. And as far as the future is concerned, everybody is in the dark.
- Refuse to make promises so that you don't set traps for yourself. There will always be opponents, critics, and subordinates who try to pin you down with promises you've made. Avoid such situations. If that fails, show

understanding for the other person's request, but explain it will take more time; you really don't know how long. Learn to prevaricate if ever promises are brought up.

- A joke can work wonders in turning a situation to your advantage. But avoid creating the impression that you're nothing but a clown.
- Don't be drawn into detail about your intentions, your aims, your approach. Instead, describe the situation you are currently involved in: "I'm in the middle of a process of evaluation and reevaluation. It is, indeed, a challenging and fascinating process." You aren't lying; nor are you telling the truth. If employees or bosses press you for details, tell them that's a good question, praise them for their insight, and stress that's why you're in the middle of a complicated process. This is a standard trick used by politicians to fill hours and hours of broadcasting time with meaningless guff.

Reputation management Never forget that the power you wield in an organization depends on your reputation. Develop ways of enhancing and honing it to suit your environment. Best of all, show qualities that others only dream about.

I once knew a man who combined a good reputation with courage. He'd taken the risk of starting his own company. It grew and grew until after a few years it employed some eight hundred people. It was a nice little company—one in which, he'd often say, he'd like to work himself.

His reputation made him an honored guest at seminars, conferences, round-table discussions, and receptions. Why? What smell did he exude? What did he cultivate with the utmost care? It was the impression that he had discovered the secret of eternal prosperity. That this secret lay largely in having the right tide and a following wind was something he preferred not to mention. It probably never even occurred to him.

This, then, is reputation management at its finest: acting out the dreams that others have. If your company demands decency and precision, make sure your suit is well pressed. If creativity and originality rule, go overboard so that people admire you for doing something others wouldn't think or dare to do. If you need to be warm and compassionate ... well, you get the picture.

But you do have to keep your reputation in check. You're allowed to go a bit further than the crowd, but not too far. I once knew a politician who couldn't get his name on the list of candidates for the upper house, despite an impressive record in government and corporate life. The reason? He was too pronounced in his opinions. His reputation was that of a man who adopted controversial positions. That didn't fit in with his party's idea of a statesman.

No matter what reputation you wish to achieve, in no matter what circle, there's one thing you must avoid at all costs: gaining the reputation of being a calculating and devious person. Always feign a degree of naiveté in all your political games. As I mentioned at the start of my letter, good rats are never recognized for the rats they are. It's not about who you are, but who you seem to be. The Romans used to say *videre non esse*.

Being unpredictable If you really want to frustrate your opponents, being unpredictable will keep up the tension. If they don't know what's happening, they'll start filling in the gaps.

One of my professors taught me a technique based on something that had happened to him. You need to know that he was disabled and used crutches. One evening in spring—the light was beautiful, it must have been around seven—he was walking through a park on his way to give a lecture.

He was slowly negotiating a gravel path at his own pace—crutch, leg, crutch, leg—when he saw some suspicious characters a little way off. By the look of it, two of those shady youths that hang around doing nothing all evening. They headed toward him. Big trouble, he thought to himself, and started weighing up his chances. Turning around and going back was out of the question; they would then be behind him. Turning off into the bushes or the lake wasn't really an option either. So—carry on.

He walks on. His opponents get nearer; shapes take on features. Uh-oh. The sun shines down on the approaching confrontation. They are only a yard apart, these boys and the professor. Everything seems to hold its breath. The mugging is imminent.

And then the professor remembers the rule about being unpredictable. In one swift movement he flings away his crutches and starts flapping his arms and shouting, "Oeaaa, oeaaa" like some crazy bird.

Silence.

The boys look at each other, turn around, and walk off. Gerald—let's give our professor a name—retrieves his crutches and continues on his way. And—could it be a coincidence?—he runs into a policeman. He stops the officer and tells him what has happened. The officer sets off in pursuit, catches the two, and takes them to the local police station.

Now, being a true scientist, Gerald is deeply interested in people (especially in two youths who'd just been about to attack him), so he follows the three of them. At the station, he asks whether he can talk to the two boys. His charm works, and he is given permission.

"Why didn't you mug me? Why did you run off?" he asks. The boys gaze at him in growing amazement. First what just happened, and now this? "Well," stuttered one of them, "you seemed a bit mad. And we don't do crazy people. It was just too weird, man."

I'll stop here, because I've told you enough to illustrate my point. This incident shows how you can transform a situation by doing something unexpected. The two boys were probably intending to mug Gerald, but his bizarre behavior threw them into confusion.

Years later, I met my old professor again at a party held to celebrate his award of an emeritus post. I told him his story remained etched in my memory. As I recounted the incident back to him, he became more and more amused. When I finished, he said: "What a wonderful story! Of course, it never happened. But it's still a wonderful story."

And so this tale of an unpredictable incident took an unpredictable turn for me. But the essence is still clear. Create tension by being unpredictable. Make yourself into an enigma. Keep situations deliberately vague.

Wiping out tracks There was once a kingdom far, far away that had a lot of large companies working on its reconstruction. The job wasn't a pot of gold for any of them. But they were able to fleece the stupid government with inflated bills, and bribe various bureaucrats to help them get around the irritating regulations. The cash flowed in.

Now you could say this is an example of real rat work and we should take our hats off to these companies. Except—oh dear!—they were stupid enough to keep double accounts of all their dealings because they were scared they would be caught in their fraudulent activities. You can screw your opponent, but not each other. Stupid, stupid.

You see, in that country there was a whistle-blower who acted out of revenge. Insiders would tell you about rumors that were going around. Every paper-shredder in the country had been sold. These shredders had been used nonstop for weeks to wipe out the tracks.

Make sure you can never be discredited. Don't leave your notes about the next coup on the copier. (I did that once, and got a black mark on my record for my manipulative nature. I took it as a compliment.) Don't use your company email for planning your next trick. Never take center stage in gossip campaigns. Never make notes that might expose your aims, strategies, and tactics. If you use a computer, don't use the one the company gave you. It's their property, and they may ask you to return it. Destroy any reels of film that show you in compromising situations. Even the great among us take defensive measures like these.

Knowing yourself One of the greatest virtues—one that every player in political arenas has written about—is the ability to understand your own weaknesses and lock them away from the grubby little paws of all the other rats around you.

One of my vices is vanity. I crave admiration, recognition, and applause. In corporate life, this can soon turn into an Achilles heel, because a talented rat can smell a chance here.

One Tuesday afternoon while I was working at home, the phone rang. It was the boss of my boss's boss. Terribly important. He apologized for calling me at home, but he was wrestling with a problem. He and his secretary could no longer see eye to eye. Things had blown up out of all proportion, and could well end in dismissal. Could I talk to her and find out what she wanted?

"The reason I'm calling you is that you really understand people. You get along well with them." My head was swelling so much I thought I'd never be able to get out the door. Far off in the recesses of my mind, alarm bells rang faintly. I managed to say that I would clear my appointments and speak to her tomorrow, but added that if it didn't work out, I would tell him.

I was clearly being hoist by the petard of my own vanity. It stank. In effect, I was being asked to provide proof about the woman's emotional instability that could later be used against her. My boss knew that all my good deeds would count for nothing, but that was beside the point. He wanted to be able to prove to the employment tribunal that he'd done everything a good employer should.

I've always appreciated this piece of manipulation because it showed me something I was unaware of, but others around me could probably see: my vanity. From that moment, I pulled down the shutters when anyone paid me compliments.

I once told this story to a very powerful man, a wheeler-dealer of the top rank. I said that I now battened down the hatches when a storm of compliments threatened. He shook his head. "That's totally wrong. If somebody comes to you to satisfy your need for compliments, you mustn't close the shutters. No, no—you should immediately think: this man or woman is dependent on me. What do I need from him or her? You shouldn't react too much, but remain slightly aloof and then come back with your own demands."

Why did it take me so long to secure a place in the verminicity master class?

6 | The Game

By now, you know all about interests, sources of power, and tactics. The moment will soon come when you'll have to pull all the strands together and take part in the game. In this section of my letter, I'll discuss the game and the processes that lie at its heart to give you a better feel for the big picture.

What makes the rat game so difficult is that the battle can often be a long-drawn-out process, so that you experience the various skirmishes as fragmentary and isolated. That's why I would advise you to take time out regularly and let the whole thing pass the review. It's exactly what directors do when studying a new play: they put all the scenes together, one after another, to get a better picture of the drama as a whole. You'll have to do this in your mind, with the added handicap of not knowing how the play will end. As with much human experience, the full story can only be told in retrospect. All the same, it's sensible to keep telling yourself what has been happening while constantly asking yourself: do I really understand it? Do I understand it now? That will keep you on course.

Transition from honesty to verminicity

Most people know exactly when they are crossing the boundary between fair play and verminicity. Years of moral training and ethical indoctrination will bear fruit. You'll notice when you cross the line because you'll become less open and weigh your words before you speak, as I explained in chapter 2.

Many people find their work becomes more demanding when they get drawn into the rat game. As one manager recently told me, "I still find my work interesting, but all those power plays sap my energy." When people start complaining that they are exhausted or demotivated, look to the political battles that are wearing them out.

Another sign that you are about to leave normal work behind is when you start asking yourself whether you should be completely honest with your boss and colleagues, or whether you might do better to fudge the issue or keep your mouth shut. If you are grappling with this problem, you should be grateful; you're probably in the middle of a situation known as the "prisoner's dilemma." I'll try to explain using a simple chart.

		BOSS	
		Open	Closed
ME	Open	*Both gain something*	*I bite the dust*
	Closed	*I get the jackpot*	*Both lose something*

Initial dilemma

Our example presumes that you and your boss are in conflict. Both of you can be open or closed about what you want. If you are open, you operate in good faith; if you are closed, you operate from distrust.

The difficulty lies in trying to decide whether your boss will be open or not. He'll face the same problem with you. What you choose to do will be informed by what you think he will do, and vice versa.

If you are open and your boss is too, you can, after a certain amount of conjecture and compromise, reach some sort of deal. Probably both of you will gain something out of the exercise. The problem arises when your boss wants you to be open while he remains closed. There's a big chance he'll use your honesty against you, and you'll lose out.

The best option for you is the reverse: when your boss is honest with you, but you aren't completely open with him. Then you'll probably be able to capitalize on his naiveté.

If both of you are equally guarded and mistrustful of each other, there's a strong chance neither of you will get what you want, and you'll both have to face some kind of loss.

You will, of course, want to know what on earth you should do with all this at work. I personally follow the rule that people have to prove their honesty. Reticence about things that really matter is for me more appropriate than absolute candor, although I admit that by nature I'm more inclined to be frank than guarded.

To sum up: if you're wondering whether you can trust another person or not, you're only a hair's breadth away from distrusting them. There are several other signs that you are about to take—or have just taken—that step from fair play to verminicity. Remember that honesty, like reputation, may arrive on foot, but it will leave on horseback.

Degrees of verminicity

The rat game can escalate quite alarmingly from covert to open hostility, and from subtle rat machinations to in-your-face techniques such as passing over people, isolating them, and subjecting them to "Big Brother" forms of repression. You don't need to reach for the big guns straightaway.

I was once given a handy categorization by a rat well schooled in corporate politics. He drew a distinction between "cunning," "sly," and "sneaky."

Anybody who operates with cunning generally earns our respect. When cunning deeds come to light, we tend to admire and take pleasure in them.

That doesn't happen with slyness. Sly people are usually shunned; they set off alarm bells of suspicion. Anybody who is sly can turn their plots and schemes against us. We keep them at a good distance and treat them with the necessary reserve.

And sneaky people? Well, they're the businessmen who set up networks of paper companies so that they can satisfy their enormous greed for money. Being sneaky doesn't earn you much respect. But don't allow yourself to be distracted by these moral considerations; it's the results that count. What you have to avoid is *getting a reputation* for being sly or sneaky. Take care to conceal your sneakiness under a cloak of integrity or cunning.

Opening gambit

Most of the rats I've known in the course of my career tell me they never go into battle unprepared. That doesn't mean, they would hasten to add, that they always get things right. Sometimes you can forget things, or ignore details you assume are irrelevant only to discover later that they were crucial.

In the opening game, you must first survey the arena and furnish it as comfortably as possible for yourself.

Assessing the situation The best rats are realpolitikers: pragmatists. In other words, they are able to review their situation soberly and dispassionately. They look at the facts and decide how much room for maneuver they have.

As you read this, you may well think that you are just such a person, and that all this goes without saying. If only that were true! Finding themselves embroiled in battle, far too many people will sound the retreat by denying that the battle is taking place—or else throw themselves wholeheartedly into the heat of battle and fight like someone possessed. Here we see the natural biological impulses that are part of our human makeup: fight or flight.

The realpolitiker, on the other hand, does something quite unnatural. He stops, faces the danger, and analyzes it. What are the factors, who are the players, how strong am I, what course am I on, what can I get out of this to further my aims? After careful consideration, he identifies the path he can most realistically follow. Even if he decides to go for broke, it will be a well-considered decision. Recklessness and bravura don't feature in a rat's vocabulary.

A man in his midforties once told me about a conflict he'd had at work. He and his three colleagues enjoyed their jobs, but their boss had decided to disband their department. He'd heard the news over the summer while he was away on vacation.

"Well," he said to me, "I took a few long walks through the Alps to calm my emotions and decide what I should do. And then I realized that fighting for my department would be futile. The company was switching to different products, we were too expensive, and the market was changing. While I was chewing this over, I realized that I'd been catapulted into a run-of-the-mill employment conflict, and that I should get as much money as possible for myself. They couldn't get rid of me that easily. I decided that was the battle I would fight. Within six months, I would make sure I had a new job and a pile of money."

This example shows us the aim of the consideration process: to make a realistic assessment of the value of favorable and unfavorable results. Such results will only have meaning for you if, from the start, you are able to associate them with what you want for yourself: your goals, desires, and interests, both short- and long-term.

How people view a conflict depends entirely on their aims, dreams, fantasies, and nightmares. Are you aiming for financial security because you have alimony debts piling up? Are you after a higher position? Perhaps you've already decided to leave the company within the next few years to start your own business? Or maybe you are an idealist with nature, animals, or your fellow human beings dear to your heart?

No matter what, the preparation you have to do when a battle begins includes answering once again the question: what do I really want? The question is pretty mundane, and the answers probably will be too. Most people already know what they want. Just make sure you have sorted everything out in your mind.

Consider conducting a brief audit of the power you and your opponent have at your disposal. Be aware how well (or how badly) equipped you are in terms of the sources I mentioned earlier.

You probably have more power than you think. Network power is the most widespread and easily tapped source. Sometimes you have to include other people in your rat game, whether they are in the same boat as you or might be useful instruments for you. If you have to take people into your confidence, always sleep on it first. Is the other person discreet, or will they tell others what you tell them? Might they turn against you?

My experience is double-edged. The good news is that a general conspiracy can lead to better plans and battles. The bad news is that you have to keep your eye on a lot more people, find out what they might and might not know, and ascertain whether they are gossiping or not.

The most dangerous people are the enthusiastic type who don't appreciate the importance of the information you are sharing with them. This has nothing to do with intelligence, social skills, or strategic acumen. I know a brilliant man in his thirties who would go a lot further in management if he knew how to curb his enthusiasm and not let things slip out inadvertently.

When you've finished your review of the impending conflict, it's time to make your first move. Push and shove can begin. The good rat is concerned with just three things: the opponent's intentions, the opponent's starting position, and the struggle to gain the initiative.

The difference between "good" and "real" reasons You have your plans, strategies, and considerations; so does your opponent. In the opening gambit, you should give this a lot of attention. You'll have to distinguish, as a member of my family once taught me, between "good" reasons and "real" reasons. Everybody in corporate life has learned to show good reasons for doing something; the real reasons normally take some tracking down.

So you will have to spy on your opponent, using those who work behind enemy lines as informants. Then you can have those face-to-face discussions using the "let's be honest" tactic. You might offer your opponent a tiny snippet of information that you blow up out of all proportion to give the impression you are taking them into your confidence. Or you might propose pseudohypothetical cases to try to lure your opponent into revealing their true intentions: imagine that things were like this—what would your position be then? Or you put yourself in someone else's position: supposing I was P., what would I do?

Wearing down In corporate conflicts, people will try to charm you or wear you down. Quite right, too. If you can deplete your opponent's energy, the struggle will be cleaner, swifter, and a good deal more comfortable.

A manager wanted to get rid of five employees simply because they cost him more than they earned for him. What's more, he had been told by the shareholders that he should get rid of any "bleeders" that were draining the company dry, so that it could be sold for a good price. The owners wanted to realize their dreams and cash in.

Knowing this could evolve into a conflict, he started negotiating with the five employees. His assessment was that everything would go smoothly, without costing too much, if he could wear them down before the conflict started.

The tactic he used, part of the manager's usual repertoire, was that of the misplaced victim. "You know," he began, "I've been carrying this around with me since the summer—no, longer, since the spring. I've given it a lot of thought and it isn't an easy matter. I'm finding all this very hard, as I'm sure you all know. But the fact is that we have to place your department at some distance from the rest of the company. If we carry on as we are, everything could go horribly wrong ...."

The five employees were silent for a moment. Then they started to ask questions. How did you feel about it? What were your reasons? Difficult problem? What can we do about it? They'd fallen for it, at least for the moment. The manager had played his cards brilliantly. He'd turned himself into a victim, and was appealing to his employees for help.

The executioner asks the condemned man to hang himself because he hates the sight of it all. There are countless other games you can play to weaken your opponent. Just follow these simple rules of thumb:

- Blacken your opponent by turning them into the villain while playing the innocent yourself.

- If you can't avoid being cast as villain, always point out the circumstances that have forced this role on you.
- Take advantage of others' misplaced loyalty. In their heart of hearts, many people are more loyal to the company than to themselves.
- Play the underdog and see if anyone steps in to be the good Samaritan or the savior.

One thing you can be sure of is that there will be an initial dispute about the nature of what's going on. Is this a conflict, a technical difference of opinion, a natural hurdle in the change process, fraternal strife, a win-win situation, or a bitter struggle from which only one side can emerge victorious?

Whether such definitions are close to the mark or figments of the imagination, I can't say. What I've noticed, however, is that people match their actions to the way they see the conflict—how they, as we have now called it for several decades, "define the situation." That's why managers prefer to talk of a win-win situation rather than a conflict. The label you use affects the emotions you feel and the actions you take.

As a rat, then, you must try to prevent your opponent getting the power to give a name to what's happening. They will always do so in a way that serves their own interests. You can't avoid doing the same. If the "win-win situation" suits you, play it that way; if "we have a serious work conflict" meets your purpose, so be it. Rats don't distinguish between true or untrue definitions; there are only useful situations and unhelpful ones.

The time has come to discuss the end game. When will the moment of truth arrive? What form will it take: a court case, a local council decision, or an approval by the board?

Don't start considering the end game too early, but do make

sure you gather evidence that may be useful when it comes. If your cards will eventually be played in front of a tribunal, you'll have to build up a dossier right from the very start, collecting material that casts your opponent in a bad light. If there are documents floating around the company that could damage you, you must track them down and destroy or alter them.

One sublime rat who was planning to start his own business discovered that his current employment contract, which contained an anticompetitive clause, had been mislaid. Now his immediate boss, a woman, was having an affair with the man who was to become his new business partner. Very handy! She would draw up a new contract—*without* the anticompetitive clause, naturally—and put it in his file. No sooner said than done.

When the two men started their new business, the company tried to stop them, citing the anticompetitive clause. Unfortunately, the only employment contract it could produce turned out not to contain one.

Artful! The end game—a court case—was anticipated superbly, the opportunities were seized, and the documents were adapted. Whether the story is morally justifiable or a case of fraud is something I'll leave to the judgment of ethicists and lawyers. My only concern is to describe a rat's behavior. The lesson is simple: anticipate in your opening gambit the moment of truth.

Somebody once taught me that you can distinguish three plans in every process. First is the plan you have drawn up in advance, setting out the direction in which you will march. Second is the intermediate plan with the adjustments you made because the path wasn't quite what you expected and you encountered unforeseen events along the way. And third is the retrospective plan, a reconstruction of events that you now call the real plan. Of course, it can be made only after everything has been completed.

The problem—and also the beauty—of this is that the three plans don't have to bear any resemblance to one another. Keep this in mind when you draw up your plans. You'll do everything at least three times.

The middle game

In the middle game, the tactics I've previously described will reveal themselves in their full glory and infinite variety. You will torment, gather your trumps, infiltrate networks to claim your pound of flesh—oops, sorry, not to claim your pound of flesh, but to achieve your aims. And then you'll work on your reputation, because it seems to be moving in a direction you don't want, and sprinkle a light dusting of insinuation to add spice to the daily dose of suspicion that you spread.

The middle game will introduce a number of aspects that are inherent in the process and may or may not be susceptible to your influence. All the more reason to discuss them in detail.

Initiative and direction My discussions with rats and my own experience have taught me that much attention should be paid to who determines the speed and nature of the battle. You'll want to control the battle throughout and restrict your opponent's retaliation to moments that suit you best.

Whether you approach the battle offensively or defensively, you'll still want to determine how the game is played. But of course your opponent wants the same thing: to define the situation, set the tempo, and get you to react to their actions. So another conflict will soon emerge: who has the initiative?

You mustn't confuse this with being proactive, a term that is frequently used in management literature to define a company's spirit (happy rows of happy workers, that sort of thing). No, for the rat, initiative is more complicated.

Often you will do nothing but lurk in the background and watch how things develop, because your assessment told you this was the best strategy. Sometimes you'll have to act decisively because the stars are favorably aligned or the ice is thick enough for skating. And if there's a threat that you'll lose the initiative, you'll have to use all your wiles to seize back control.

Imagine that your boss asks you to think about ways of reorganizing your department. He says, "Can't we think about introducing a new governance model?" This is refined language for: we're going to have to work differently, people will have to go, your working conditions will deteriorate, and you may lose your job to boot.

First of all, let's pay tribute to your manager's rhetorical astuteness. He has a nice turn of phrase. What normal people would define as an employment conflict, he has already defined as a technical problem. By using this opening, he tries to take control of the situation and seize the initiative.

If you acquiesce, he'll start handing out roles by asking you to draw up a concrete proposal—a smart move. If you comply, you accept his definition of the situation. You do what he wants you to do; he, meanwhile, can retreat to a safe distance. He can lean back in his chair and scrutinize your proposals, criticize them and say yes or no. He has become the leader of the conflict.

You can bet your bottom dollar he'll move the situation in the direction that best serves his interests. And you won't be able to condemn him, because that would mean playing the role of victim, something good rats would never permit themselves to do. You'd do much better to follow his example. An experienced rat tries to regain the initiative as quickly as possible.

You can send the ball back into his court by saying something like this: "All these developments sound really interesting. I realize you have big plans and want to achieve a great deal. I would enjoy working with you on this based on a concrete proposal from you. I don't think I could say anything useful until then."

In this way, you tell him, very politely, that it's his problem and you're prepared only to react to his proposals in retrospect. He'll probably make a few more attempts to get you to change your mind: "You could start by offering some suggestions. That would give the plan greater consensus."

Of course you want to think about things and work on them—feign willingness—but in a meaningful way: on the basis of a concrete proposal. At this point, you have wrested the initiative from him. You've put him to work and placed the responsibility back on his shoulders. Now you can wait until he comes back to you with something.

You've written down what you discussed and had him initial it: no possibility of escape. And if he takes too long coming back to you, send him a polite email asking if everything is OK and if he has already sent something to you that might have gone astray. In this way, you keep your grip on the process. Naturally, you make a copy of the email and file it away in your dossier, because it shows how carelessly your manager treats you.

Hasten and delay In more complex struggles, you'll have to do a lot of preparation behind the scenes before you can make a move. This means you'll have to control the speed of the moves. You set the beat; you're the conductor.

Can you always do that? No. Sometimes your opponent is more powerful than you, and unexpected events crop up. But every organization has mechanisms that can hasten or delay. Use them to set the tempo you need for your master stroke.

An adviser was given the job of merging two feuding committees. He had to get grown-up men and women to work together—people who, after long and successful careers in their fields, had developed all the brainpower of deep-frozen chickens. He couldn't discuss the pros and cons of working together with them in the usual way. That would achieve nothing.

The only solution was to create a situation in which the pain and suffering of not merging would be greater than working with your worst enemy. He would play the game of eliminating alternatives until only two evils remained, and the lesser of the two was the result he needed.

So he bombarded both committees with questions that needed decisions—decisions that could be taken only after consultation with the other committee. In the end, they had to hold three extra meetings a week to cope with them all. This tactic called for exceptional orchestration and close attention to tempo. The bombardment lasted for two months. Troops had to be mobilized; the questions couldn't originate from the adviser because that would be too obvious. And in the second month, the flow of questions would have to speed up to prevent routine setting in and keep the committees in a constant state of frustration.

Toward the end, our rat had to slow the tempo when two committee members went out of commission: one suffered a broken bone, the other, a bereavement. So paucity took over from excess.

This example illustrates the important role of time in a merger. Speed up, slow down.

Orchestration When you're fighting in a company, it can be advisable to orchestrate your actions. Sometimes it isn't wise to take the solo part. A humble place among the second violins is much more suitable for a rat.

A prominent place may well encourage your opponent to point a finger in your direction and claim you are playing the wrong notes. Remember that your opponents will want to know who *their* opponents are so that they can anticipate their actions. Fleeting associations, unexpected alliances, and hazy boundaries between those who support them and those who oppose them will be anathema.

This emerged clearly in a recent conflict, one of the largest ever in the Dutch transportation industry. All at once, a number of collectives arose spontaneously, outside the usual realm of trade unions and general consultation bodies. Organizing themselves using cellphones and the Internet, and meeting everywhere and nowhere, they took independent actions that wreaked havoc. Panic gripped the employers, the government, and the unions. Who are we fighting here?

Anything that happens on a large scale can happen on a small scale too. Ensure that in any work conflict, you are the one who orchestrates everything. Let your colleague have their say, and then say something yourself. Decide who sends out a letter. Agree who will start a lobby. Modern communications technology makes it easy to arrange appointments and reach agreements.

I once orchestrated every word and deed in a work conflict. It didn't seem sensible to do it all myself. During the postmortem with my opponent—we concluded our business as friends—he said he constantly had the feeling that the whole thing had been orchestrated: there was that telephone call, then that letter, then that email. He thought it remarkably clever, and asked whether it was true.

At the time, I simply smiled and gave an evasive answer. I can tell you now that nothing was wrong with his intuition.

Good luck, bad luck No matter how calculating you are, or how well you plan and predict, you'll always need a bit of good luck. And you're bound to run into bad luck too. The exact nature of good luck, bad luck, and coincidence is something I'll leave to philosophers and mystics. Courses in miracles are wasted on me. But at the same time, I don't let them bother me: coincidences can't be orchestrated. They happen, or they don't.

A totally different issue—and one in which I *am* deeply interested—is whether you can make good use of coincidences. Of course you can! Look out for any unexpected incidents and immediately harness them for your cause. Perhaps it is this nose for exploiting chance events that distinguishes a great rat from a mediocre one.

Take, for example, the former mayor of N——, who's involved in an ongoing conflict with the councilman for urban planning. The councilman—one of those go-getters with dandruff on his collar—knows exactly how to offend every single person involved in a major construction project. There's talk of a budget deficit. The council has made mistakes that the press hasn't yet uncovered. Bureaucrats, contractors, and directors have been hounded. Local government at its saddest.

Seeking a way out of the problems, the main players have agreed not to speak to the press. Despite their differences, they all agree it is the enemy, responsible for inciting and publicizing the scandals. You might think that having discovered something they can agree on, it shouldn't be too difficult to stick to the agreement. Not at all: just two days later, that scumbag of a councilman gives an extensive interview to the local newspaper. Headlines on page three.

And then the mayor revealed his true talent as organizer and rat. He went straight to the councilman's office and took the building project out of his portfolio. By giving an interview, the councilman had become a central element in the conflict. It was vital to find an administrative solution to the problem, and he, the mayor, would find one.

This is making good use of a chance event—in this case, the councilman's stupid move. The mayor hadn't laid a trap for his opponent, nor predicted what he might do. But when the barbecued chicken fluttered by, all he had to do was snatch it out of the air while the councilman looked on, powerless. The councilman was reduced to the role of observer; the mayor became the director.

Many other examples from corporate and administrative circles bear out the importance of a nose for chance events. What all rats have in common is that they have a crystal-clear picture of what they are striving for. Anything that comes their way is judged by its usefulness to their mission: a telephone call, an aside in a brief conversation at a noisy reception, an NB in an email, an interview, a piece of gossip. By such things are careers made and broken.

I recently heard a sad story about a councilman and party leader who held top-secret discussions with an environmental party after the local elections. He was trying to find out whether it would be possible to form a coalition with them because his ultimate career objective was to oust the Citizens' Interest Party (CIP) from its traditional seat in the local council.

One afternoon, in a secluded wood far from the council's boundaries, the councilman is sitting on a terrace enjoying a beer with representatives of the environmental group when who should cycle by but one of the CIP members on an afternoon out. When the CIP chairman got to hear about this, his joy was unconfined. He'd been looking for a way to get rid of this councilman for years.

During the next council meeting, the CIP chairman attacked the councilman for conducting his own little discussions behind everybody's back.

"At that moment, silence descended over the meeting. A shock rippled through the room, and through me. I realized at that moment that my party was going to let me fall. Just like that. In a few seconds. This would appear in the paper. I had disgraced the party. It was going to cost me my skin.

"The next morning, the party had a meeting. The atmosphere was chilling. People I had known for years ignored me. I couldn't keep my position. I asked them whether they still had confidence in me. Silence. I drew my conclusions, and in the meeting the next day, I announced my resignation." Coincidences can also prove unlucky.

Impatience, cowardice, and battle fatigue The rat game is filled with emotions. Some are useful because they help you progress in the game: anger, happiness about an unexpected chance, the righteous feeling of a just battle. Others stop you moving forward. You're sure to come up against counterproductive emotions. The art is learning how to deal with them.

Impatience I've known many rats who were masterful in their ability to analyze and develop strategies, but ultimately failed because they were unable to control their impatience. They

146

wanted a lot—and they wanted it now. They couldn't accept the fact that things develop at their own pace. Your opponent may have to think about the situation, an adversary may be lying in wait for you, organizations don't move fast, and chances don't present themselves on cue.

I must admit to impatience in my own battles. I want to get them out of the way: I've analyzed everything and made the moves, and now I have to wait, and wait, and wait. The danger is that you take steps—calling people, writing to them, spreading extra gossip—to speed things up. Resist! Don't rush things along unless you're convinced it will help your cause, and not just allay your impatience. When you act out of emotion rather than calculation and fail to make proper appraisals, things are bound to go wrong.

The keyword here is acceptance: you must accept both the slowness with which things happen and your own impatience. But how can you accept that prickling sensation that makes you jumpy, stops you concentrating, and urges you to act?

I can't offer you anything but common-sense remedies. Some people take walks in the open air. Others swear by diversions and throw themselves into their work, their hobbies, or their relationship. Some choose to talk things through with people they trust to try and get them in perspective. Me? Well, in my moments of impatience, I take down the Bible and read Ecclesiastes 3. It says that for everything there is a season, a time for every purpose under the heaven, a time to build and to destroy, a time to love and to hate, to be born and to die.

You'll have to find out for yourself which remedies can help you avoid acting on your impatience and rushing into ill-considered deeds.

Cowardice If you want to be a rat, you need courage. This is what some people miss. They worry about the damage they could suffer if things go wrong, and so they screw up.

I've already written about fear: of defeat, failure, rejection. In your battles, you'll have to face these fears in all their many guises: as doubt (am I doing the right thing?), as dejection (why am I doing this?), as perfectionism (do I have everything under control?), as ethics (can I really do this?), as ... Fear is a thousand-headed monster that can smell when it can make you its prey.

You are cowardly when you most fear the consequences for yourself. The battle could lead to your dismissal, your defeat, your disgrace. You have to distinguish between withdrawing from battle because you can't possibly win, and retreating because you are afraid of defeat even though it isn't inevitable. That's what I would call cowardice.

Imagine a sportsman who is as successful in business as he is on the sports field. He rises quickly to the top of the most innovative companies. People consider him an authority. He is awarded an honorary professorship. And yet he regularly leaves the companies he works for. Is he a coward? Is he impatient? No. He probably has a well-developed nose for lost causes and leaves the battlefield promptly so that he isn't injured by the fallout. Does that make him a coward? No. He's smart because he knows when the time has come to quit the arena.

What should you do about fears that occur during the battle? I suggest you take them seriously. Fear is always a signal that there's a threat around. The problem isn't the signal, but how you interpret it: is it a false alarm, a warning light, or a red alert?

Your feeling of fear won't answer these questions. That's why you have to return to your assessments, your stories, your analyses. We all know that reason, the mind, is the only thing that can confirm or deny your fear. Look on fear as a suspicion, a hypothesis; that way you can gain the most from it.

Fortunately, the threats in corporate life don't require an immediate response. There is always time to react—time you can put to good use to weigh your options.

Battle fatigue And then you fall out of the arena of events where reaction follows action, plans are made, victories celebrated, wounds tended. You fall into a space where there is nothing: no time, experience, pleasure, anger, or even hate.* There is only the soft hum of despondency. A sense of futility—"Why on earth should I?"—echoes through the mind. And then even that disappears. You're dejected. Nothing matters anymore. You've hidden yourself away. You're left to rot. A living fossil. After long conflicts, your struggles for power in one arena after another, and the interminable rat race, you're fatigued; the days weigh on you.

This is part of the rat's life, and a regular part too. Someone once told me: "I'd like to spend some time doing *nice* things. Working on the future with other people. Doing some networking. Undertaking new things. And no more fights. But I can't. I just don't have the energy."

Of the three negative emotions we are discussing here, battle fatigue is the most dangerous. When faced with impatience or cowardice, you can retrace your steps and use your powers of reasoning, but with battle fatigue the root of the emotion remains no matter what interpretation you give it: a conflict is just a conflict; verminicity is just verminicity. For this reason, many managers, directors, and administrators look outside the battlefield for sustenance: they play with trains, blow into

---

*For further reading I recommend Emil Corian, *The Temptation to Exist*, Times Books, 1972. Corian writes about the darker side of humanity.

didgeridoos, amble through alpine meadows, whittle wood.

At a certain point, battle fatigue reaches such proportions that rats leave the arena for good and concentrate on these uncomplicated and soul-enriching activities. "Enough is enough," they sigh. "It's over." Anybody who can't say that, whose life as a rat is not yet over, must find their bowl of warm water in which to soothe their tired feet. They must look for nonthreatening activities; nice things. That's my advice to you: seek quiet pursuits far away from the organization in which you spend so much of your time.

End game

The supreme moment; the moment of truth. Most rat battles lead to a denouement. Trump cards are played. The new order is ushered in. During long wars, you'll notice that there are many moments like this, because life is a constant struggle, and, like a successful soap, it consists of many episodes. Denouements are little more than semicolons in the chapters that are being written.

Can you see this moment approaching? Does the scent of the final battle fill the air? Or does the end emerge unannounced, like a terrorist attack? No, not that last one: you can always see the end drawing nigh. In my experience, and that of the many people I've asked about this, those in the know can usually tell when the end game has begun. And I do mean "those in the know." For the troops, those who depend on second- and thirdhand information, the moment of truth strikes like a thunderbolt. But that's because they don't have a complete picture of what's going on.

Most end games are decided in some gathering, conference, or reception during which the course of history is tweaked a little—or utterly transformed. This is where the cards that have been collected in the middle game are finally played.

Don't kid yourself that the result of these meetings depends on the force of the arguments deployed. Not at all. Everything revolves around the person with the most power: the one who can impose their will most forcefully on those around them. Dexterity can sometimes squeeze a bit more out of the end game, but the general rule is this: all the work is done in the middle game, but the results don't materialize until the end game.

The director of a recently privatized monopoly was given the job of mobilizing the forces and turning desk-bound bureaucrats into go-getting entrepreneurs. As you can imagine, that's not the kind of change that happens overnight. What he did first was to gain the support of the court. He made his preparations using work groups, lobbies, carrots, and sticks.

The moment of truth was to be the general management meeting where he would finally reveal his plans, mission, and vision to his subordinates and seek their support and loyalty. It was a tense moment. Would they back him, or try to hold things up?

Of course they supported him. He had carefully paved the way for his revolution in the palace corridors. His power was now unassailable. All he needed was official approval.

Then there was the case of the group based on a philosophical/religious interest. Strife was raging between moderate and radical factions on its committee. Nobody could remember what had started it all, but one thing was clear: the other faction had to give way. And because both factions thought exactly the same way, a fight ensued that enraged everybody.

All the players had been collecting as many trump cards as they could during the middle game, through backstabbing, gossip, pseudointellectual arguments, flattery, persuasion, and propaganda. They waited for the annual congress to play their cards. For all their talk of reason and humanity, each one of them was a remarkably talented rat of the kind we admire so much.

And so one Saturday D-Day arrived: the Day of Judgment, apocalypse now. Heated discussions, yelling, raging; the will for power lent wings to their words. Finally, votes of no confidence. Heads rolled.

Once the moment of truth had passed, those present came to their senses. As the smoke dispersed, they stared at the corpses strewn across the stage. For a moment, they felt distanced from the turmoil that had just raged before them.

Not all denouements are so dramatic. Some are no more than a chairman's hammer in a board meeting: a new road delayed, a bar license withheld. But whether you plan an event yourself or direct your energies at some decision in a boardroom or council chamber, that won't be where the struggle for power is played out. Here it will, at the most, be approved. In the supreme moment, all your homework, all your past labors, will come to fruition.

Winning and losing

Every fight must end in a decision. Unfortunately, you can't always win. Even the most gifted director, the most cunning entrepreneur, the shrewdest trade union official, will occasionally fall flat on their face.

The art is knowing how to win or lose with dignity and grace. Why bother? Because in our global village, we are certain to bump into each other again at some time or another. Today's loser is tomorrow's victor. Today's adversary is tomorrow's ally.

If you win, you'll feel triumphant. You can't help it, so enjoy it. But don't let it take you over, especially if you're in the company of people who don't share your confidences.

You may want to kick your opponent one last time, simply because you can. Beware! Do this and you sow—as we've learned through the centuries—the seeds of suspicion, enmity, and hate. Instead, disarm your opponent with a friendly word. Show that you're reasonable and don't bear a grudge. Think "togetherness."

Remember that many observers don't like seeing people kicked when they are down. People know when the battle has been won and rat tactics are no longer appropriate. They'll accuse you of cruelty, be more on their guard than ever before, and maybe start directing undermining tactics at you.

And there's another reason to be reticent about your victory: if you aren't, you'll reveal yourself as the rat you are, somebody who has the power game down to a fine art. That won't do your image much good. People will consign you to the rats' hall of fame.

So much for being a dignified winner, but you'll need to be a dignified loser too. It's no use bellyaching about losing. If you're chairman of the board, don't give an interview complaining that your employees sabotage your plans, stop you meeting your targets, and leave you to shoulder the blame. Avoid whingeing at all costs; you'll only show yourself up as a bad loser.

By all means accuse yourself of stupidity, blame yourself for incompetence, or tear your hair out for your naiveté, but never ever reproach your opponent for playing the game better than you did. Most managers, directors, and administrators find this an alien concept. They're just bad losers. People can tell what all that protesting and moaning is about. They just shrug and say: "Then you shouldn't have got into a fight." You must only play the victim if it might profit you in the next round. Preemptive victimhood is permissible.

If you lose, better to leave the ship than stay aboard. Don't be too scared of doing this, although most managers and directors are. No, I'll be more emphatic: if you lose, you should get out. Your opponent will always hold sway over you; you've shown that you are less powerful; the irritation will haunt you for years; and every action you take will be smothered by the wet blanket of your bad reputation.

Most professionals who quit make prior arrangements. I recommend you follow their example. Make sure you always have a plan B ready in case you lose. What will you do if things go wrong? Which golden handshake can you expect? Which options can you cash in? Have you ever seen a well-known politician or businessperson selling a street newspaper outside Wal-Mart? Well then ...

What's the most undignified thing you can do as a loser? What can we only speak of in whispers because it is so unworthy of a rat? What makes us feel so queasy that we'd rather ignore it? Reporting in sick!

Imagine you are a top bureaucrat with a long and notable career. You know more about what's happening in the country than almost anybody else. And then you come into conflict with your deputy secretary—no, the whole government. Nothing wrong with that, you'd say.

But imagine you lose the battle. What do you do? You resign, hold your head high, and if necessary eat dry crusts. What you *don't* do is report in sick the next day. Anything but that. I know what you're thinking: "Surely this doesn't happen? Surely there aren't any rats who would report in sick after being defeated? Not at the very top. Tell me it can't be true ..."

I hold my peace and hang my head in deepest shame.

7 | Surfing to Tradition

In the previous parts of my letter, I've taken you through the craft and practical work of the rat. In this more abstract section, I'd like to consider to whom or what we owe the political game. Who are our predecessors? Where did the rats get it all from? Surely they must be part of a tradition?

If you agree, I'll surf in an impressionistic way to some of the highlights of what I'll call, in the philosophical tradition, "the will for power." You'll understand that as with any surfing, there's an element of chance in all this. Have we visited the best, most spectacular, most important sites? We'll never know. I've allowed myself to make use of things I happened upon that looked interesting enough to throw new light on how to be a rat.

Thoughts about power

Have you ever thought how remarkable it is that we can think and talk about political games like those I've described here? I'm not talking about technical or writing ability, but about the actual terms we use. When did we first become aware of power? When did we start thinking about it?

As far as I'm concerned, we can go back to the moment when somebody realized people could get more food by cultivating land for crops than by foraging or hunting.

The advent of farming had several unforeseen side effects. As food surpluses accumulated, markets developed, and trading began, we started building cities. Then cities started to compete and wage war on one another, so we had to think about keeping the peace. Governing classes arose, and huddled together.

What made cities special was that people didn't live in them because of family or tribal connections, but simply because they happened to have their home there. So questions arose about how best to govern such places. What is sensible? What is wise?

Thus were born the first treatises about politics, power, and governance; about what is right, and what can go wrong. One of the first and most famous accounts is Plato's *Republic*. In it, he describes his ideal city-state (about the size of a small company today): what it looks like, how it should be governed, and what qualities the governor needs.

Alongside his ideal, which he calls an *aristocracy*, Plato sets four other models that he rejects as impoverished: timocracy, oligarchy, democracy, and tyranny. For rats, these failures are much more interesting than the ideal, because they allow us to learn and hone our fighting skills.

In a *timocracy*, harmony barely exists. Groups fight with each other for honor and wealth. The same is true of an *oligarchy*, only more so. Personal wealth determines whether or not you have any say in matters. In modern terms, your share portfolio takes precedence over your right to vote.

Plato also dismisses *democracy*. If too many citizens have their say, they'll fight for their own interests and acquire a taste for power. The result can only be anarchy, with everyone up in arms against everyone else. It's just like listening to your average manager talking about corporate democracy.

Neither does the last model, *tyranny*, earn any sympathy from Plato. The mark of a tyrant is that he holds absolute power. That can't produce anything worth while; it can lead only to a capriciousness that will eventually damage the general good.

Plato chooses for his utopia a state headed by (surprise!) a philosopher. The philosopher's knowledge of what is good, beautiful, and true equips him to guide everyone along the right lines. Many professionals who set great store by their superior knowledge of governance will find this concept appealing.

There's a lot more we could discuss in Plato's *Republic*, but what concerns me is his detailed and polished model of power and knowledge. No matter how practical we may be as rats, we always use some model or other to organize our company and our activities. That we can discuss organizations in terms of battlegrounds, clusters of interests, and hives of intrigue is all down to the political model-builders among whom Plato was one of the first.

Fighting with words and images

You'll remember that I made a distinction between a battle of words and a battle of fists. The first I regard as part of the rat's arsenal; the second I consider the province of fools. This distinction was drawn some 3,500 years ago in Greece. You were given lessons in both rhetoric and warfare.

Rhetoric was part of your basic political education: an important governance skill, just as it is for today's rat. You learned all kinds of oratorical techniques and familiarized yourself with the principle of rhetoric: it isn't about speaking the truth, but about channeling the hearts and minds of others in a direction you consider desirable. It's still taught in many of our modern curricula, except that now it's called advertising, PR, internal communications, change management, and how to be a rat.

What was the Greeks' rhetorical training like? In the first century AD, the philosopher Quintilian wrote *Institutio Oratoria*, a book about training to be an orator. He says you must start young. If you are chosen for an apprenticeship, you are given special exercises and games, and trained in the various tasks of the orator. You have to prepare by searching for thoughts, images, and facts. You learn to order your material in such a way as to make the strongest impact on the listener. You draw on a range of stylistic devices: imagery, contraction, hyperbole, contrast. You use auditory aids: rhythm, timbre, accent, beat.

And since an orator or rhetorician must appear on stage, you must also learn how to act, how to dress, and how to gesture. All your dramatic qualities are brought out so that you can achieve what your clients are paying for: the desired effect on others.

You'll have recognized in this summary much that is now included in presentation and communication training. We owe a great deal to the practitioners and trainers of rhetoric, for they have been enormously helpful in our manipulation of employees, bosses, and customers. The rat owes much of its vision to them.

Anyone who's prepared to claim that a company's mission is anything more than rhetoric should be off doing something else. And every colleague, manager, subordinate, guru, or consultant who comes to us with the umpteenth factual analysis of the market, the trends, the customer, and the company—each one of them should be greeted with the utmost suspicion, because we must assume that truth is once again being used as a rhetorical weapon. But if, on the other hand, you can destroy somebody else through rhetoric, by all means go ahead.

Reducing variation

In this letter, I've talked about reducing your opponent's range of choices, and given you examples. This is a well-worn theme in the struggle for power. One definition of a ruler is that he is somebody who can restrict others' behavior in order to achieve his own ends.

One of the best examples I know can be found in the emergence and spread of Christianity. Here we can find reduction techniques that are still applied in management theory today. When the new religion spread around the Mediterranean, a number of variations—theological, liturgical, and constitutional—developed in different regions. Was Jesus the Son of God or just a man, albeit a holy one? Did you need to be ordained in order to hold Mass? Should a growing, thriving church be ruled from the center or locally?

Such matters gave rise to intense divisions in the early Christian Church. In his readable study of the Vatican and the organization of the Roman Catholic Church, Thomas Reese alludes to the factors involved: fear that it might be split up into smaller churches, fear of a loss of unity, and fear of disintegration.* The measures that were debated at the time and subsequently introduced all shared the same characteristic: they reduced variation.

There followed a succession of standardization rules, as if the church were some mighty multinational. Canonical books were introduced; rules were laid down for the accreditation of those who performed certain ceremonial roles; the priesthood was created; Latin was designated as the language of liturgy; and a format was introduced for gatherings. In today's refined language, we would say that the organization used mission, vision, and standardized procedures and reports to try to get everybody moving in the same direction and block any possibility of spontaneous variation.

For us rats, this tradition is important. Our task is to broaden the possibilities open to us while reducing those available to others. And if bosses and their advisers pester us with their company visions, missions, and values, then we

---

Inside the Vatican: The politics and organization of the Catholic Church, Thomas J. Reese, Harvard University Press, 1998.

should shout: "So—you're trying to limit my variations!" As long as this suits our interests, there's nothing to worry about. But if it is against our interests and restricts our actions, then let the rat begin the game.

Development of craftsmanship

You'll have read that verminicity calls for considerable craftsmanship in understanding and analyzing arenas, interests, sources of power, tactics, and the big picture. For us, it's fairly normal to talk about such things, even though we tend to use refined language. Yet the skills are relatively new and only recently documented. To see that, let's go back five hundred years or so.

We've arrived in a seething Europe. Trade flourishes as never before; new inventions like printing are starting to change the world. In the centers of power, people chatter about the new sea routes the Portuguese are trying to discover so that they can import Asian spices more cheaply and break the monopoly of the Venetian traders. In Sagres, on the edge of the continent, a new kind of institution has been founded to document the knowledge of sailors and mapmakers. Just as scientists across the globe were to try to map the human genome some five centuries later, so here, on a sunny shore in southwestern Europe, they are endeavoring to map the seas, but with a single aim in mind: to chart a safe course to the riches of Africa and Asia.

Europe is alive—and I won't even mention the innovations in painting, the new architecture, the philosophers whose essays bring together heart and mind. We have to zoom in on one man who understands the game of power like no other, and even writes about it: Niccolò Machiavelli (1469–1527), the opportunist and oh so human (perhaps *too* human) thinker.

160

Anybody who follows his story will recognize the turbulence of Italy at that time. Tourists who visit the honeypots of Tuscany, Rome, and Naples today will find it hard to believe that Machiavelli's Italy bore a passing resemblance to twenty-first century Afghanistan. It was a country hopelessly divided, torn apart by bitter combat between domestic and foreign warlords and power-hungry clerics.

Who is in control of Florence, Milan, Rome? What wars are being waged? Is it true that new armies are being drafted? Has the government of Florence been deposed? Is it true the members have fled? What foreign interventions can we now expect? Is France our enemy or our friend? It doesn't take much imagination to realize that noblemen, citizens, and clerics would all be asking questions like these.

Amid the turmoil, Machiavelli proved to be the right man in the right place at the right time. He had the talent to analyze this nest of vipers, understand the hidden agendas of the various parties, formulate a hypothesis about their intentions, and draw up his own plans. And in 1498, because his talent was recognized by the real rulers—and probably because he had arranged his piggyback ride very cleverly—Machiavelli was appointed to a plum job: secretary to the second chancellery of the republic of Florence, a function that we might now call deputy secretary of a government department, the highest position a government official could attain. Because political leaders changed as often as they do now, while government officials kept their posts, the knowledge and experience built up by officials represented a key source of power.

Machiavelli kept his powerful position for 14 years. His job was to provide his superiors with reports about conditions in and around Florence, but he was also required to undertake diplomatic work. He was regularly dispatched as ambassador to the courts of Europe, and to the main army depots so that he could judge whether they might pose a threat to Florence.

As Frans van Dooren writes in the introduction to his Dutch translation of *The Prince:* "He combined the things he already knew with the things he heard; he analyzed the remarks that were made and the conversations at which he was present; he penetrated the psychological and human background of the events."* Here in a nutshell is Machiavelli's greatest talent, and the essence of the rat: the analysis of hidden meanings.

And yet the career of this trailblazing rat didn't come to a happy end. In 1512, the Medicis, the bankers who had run Florence until 1492, returned to power in the wake of a series of intrigues. Just as we see today when there's a change at the top, the court had to leave the stage; the new rulers wanted fresh eyes and ears that they could trust.

And so Machiavelli was dismissed. After spending some time in prison, he returned to his farm in the Tuscan hills and wrote *The Prince.* In it he describes how to acquire, hold on to, and increase power. He does this by giving tips on how people should react under certain circumstances.

I'd like to mention four aspects of Machiavelli's thinking that I've dealt with in this letter. First is his *pessimism*. Anybody who looks at the world through his eyes can't escape from a sense of gloom and disappointment:

"Because this is to be asserted in general of men, that they are ungrateful, fickle, false, cowardly, covetous, and as long as you succeed they are yours entirely; they will offer you their blood, property, life, and children, as is said above, when

---

*Athenaeum-Polak & Van Gennep, Amsterdam, 1976; since publication, the translation has been reprinted regularly.

the need is far distant; but when it approaches they turn against you."*

Second, Machiavelli's thinking is *amoral*. I'm not saying that amorality should always figure prominently in our activities today, but it's refreshing to set aside our usual refined manners and analyze companies and organizations amorally and rudely:

"And you have to understand this, that a prince, especially a new one, cannot observe all those things for which men are esteemed, being often forced, in order to maintain the state, to act contrary to fidelity, friendship, humanity, and religion. Therefore it is necessary for him to have a mind ready to turn itself accordingly as the winds and variations of fortune force it, yet, as I have said above, not to diverge from the good if he can avoid doing so, but, if compelled, then to know how to set about it."

This kind of language is no longer used at conferences and seminars. We can hear echoes of secrets that we no longer speak about but still use in our daily work.

Third, I'd like to stress Machiavelli's *common sense*. He makes it abundantly clear that he's concerned not with the fantasies people may have about power, but with the thing itself. He watches what people actually do in the political game and transforms it into a down-to-earth practical guide.

His analyses are not, as is so often the case today, tainted by blame or by foolish optimism that everything will soon be much better. As he says, "But, it being my intention to write a thing which shall be useful to him who apprehends it, it appears to me more appropriate to follow up the real truth of the matter than the imagination of it."

---

*Quotations are taken from Niccolò Machiavelli, *The Prince*, New Albion Press e-book.

And finally, Machiavelli has a sharp eye for *coincidences*. He knows that rulers must watch out for the whims of fate so that they can adapt to them where necessary: "I believe also that he will be successful who directs his actions according to the spirit of the times, and that he whose actions do not accord with the times will not be successful."

With that last quotation, we must take our leave of Renaissance Italy and bid farewell to a man who played a vital part in the rat's evolution.

Eliminating the impure

A large part of our rat repertoire is of a more recent date, having been developed in the prisons, asylums, and hospitals of the eighteenth and nineteenth centuries. When we ask employees to take a personality test, provide 360° feedback, or attend a development center, we are making use of the diligent pioneering work of doctors, prison wardens, psychiatrists, and hygienists a couple of hundred years ago.

The instruments we use to expose people's deep-seated personality traits, their performance, their competencies, their potential—in fact, all those analytical processes that we now consider perfectly normal—are the product of work with criminals, lunatics, the sick, and the unskilled. And they have lost none of their power.

Let us first pause to take a look at this struggle against impurity.* First, the hospitals. There can be no greater contrast imaginable than between yesterday's sanitarium and today's hospital as it gradually takes on every aspect of an airport (including the arrival and departure lounges). In the sanitarium, all the sick were kept together in one place—apart from those

---

*I base my remarks here on the work of the French philosopher Michel Foucault (1926–84).

unfortunates with contagious illnesses who weren't allowed in in the first place. The modern hospital returns to the concept of the early clinics, where people started putting lungs with lungs and stomachs with stomachs. Illnesses were classified according to the parts of the body they affected.

This compartmentalization is not just conceptual, but physical. If you walk through a lung ward, it will be filled with people suffering from lung diseases. By organizing the sick in this way, doctors hoped to obtain better reference material to help them develop better therapies.

The same is true of prisons. The French philosopher Michel Foucault, in his magnificent work on the emergence of the modern prison, highlights the changes that have occurred over the centuries.* Anyone who broke the law used to be locked away with fellow criminals in some deep dungeon. If you've seen the movie *Midnight Express*, you can probably imagine all too well what conditions were like.

But at some point during the eighteenth century, people started building different prisons in Europe. Prisoners were locked up in individual cells, put under guard, and subjected to a rigorous program of activities. The aim was to turn criminals into nice, friendly, law-abiding citizens.

And then there was psychiatry. During the nineteenth century, a new group of specialists emerged and began to map the human mind in all its variety. A series of classifications was developed; a growing number of psychiatric illnesses were identified, named, and charted like the elements in the periodic table. The measurement of madness had begun.

During the same period, enlightened citizens started to worry about the poverty and filth that industrialization was spreading

---

Discipline and Punish: The birth of the prison, Vintage, 1995

through society. Factories spewed out black smoke that hung in the sky. Cities stank. Infection and revolution threatened.

A great civilizing drive began. Sewers were laid, better infant care helped control the population, medical services were set up, and when new houses were built, they had separate small kitchens, forcing people to eat politely and properly in the living room.

All efforts were directed at banning the unhygienic and impure. "Impure" meant anything that wasn't planned or under control: chance, disease, insanity, the irrational, the lascivious. In other words, everything that could be done to reduce autonomous variation was done.

As we saw earlier, modern companies still make use of these hygiene measures. We analyze, measure, and research our employees, bosses, and customers, and put them into pigeonholes. Our ability to subject people to wholesale investigation comes courtesy of the work of the classifiers and measurement freaks of the past 150 years. And professionals, trendy consultancies, and eccentric professors are still devising new audits, controls, classifications, methodologies, assessments, and monitoring systems. All are designed to subjugate other people utterly, and to gain and maintain control over any deviation from the norm.

It's all a battle

The grumpy Greek philosopher Heraclitus is generally credited as being the first exponent of the notion that everything's a struggle. In the few remaining fragments of his work, he writes that the origin of the world, and of gods and people, stems from the primordial force that we can best describe as "battle" or "conflict."

Everything is the result of a collision of opposites: water and fire, god and god, god and man, man and man. Because of that, all is flux. Conflict is everywhere.

I'd now like to bring us to the last thread in our theme. If we are no more than rats, surely we are following our most primitive instincts, obeying our most deep-seated urge? As socially aware individuals, can we act otherwise? Let's look at three different schools of thought that may help us decide whether our destiny is to be a rat.

Social dependencies Let's call the first school of thought that we encounter sociology. Under this heading we bring together all the various philosophies that tell us we are involved in conflict and cooperation because we are social animals. We depend on each other for survival, and to enjoy a good life. That was true for the hunter-gatherers, and it's still true in our networked society today.

The self-contained man—autonomous, independent, proud, and able to control his own virtues and vices—sets himself apart from mere mortals, and is free from all interests and desires. Such a man may exist in fairy tales or epics, but not in everyday life. Even the financially independent need to visit a Wal-Mart to buy food, or frequent some three-star restaurant. We are all dependent on one another. Anybody who lives and works in modern society is part of a long chain of interdependencies, as the German sociologist Norbert Elias pointed out.

This perspective is particularly useful if we want to understand exactly what goes on in today's organizations. All at once we can see chains of interdependencies between relatively autonomous units. Each pursues its own interests and aims, but will work with others when it is to their mutual benefit. Equally, it will fight them when the zero-sum game—where the victory of one will mean the defeat of the other—rears its head. Ruling such a chain of interdependencies involves barter, pestering, interference, threats, seduction, alliances, and banishment.

This is also true of modern network-style organizations, only more so. Professionals from top to bottom are soon drawn into the processes of mutual influence and manipulation. And this power play—because that's what I would call it—is no longer reserved for our elders and betters; no, these days younger and younger businesspeople are confronted with the kind of thing that used to be played out behind closed boardroom doors.

All this may create an impression of amiable and egalitarian business groups, practices, or whatever the trendy term may be, filled with eager youths and experienced elders, all working together as individual entrepreneurs. Yet let's not forget that there are always people in such chains of interdependencies who have more to offer than others.*

The conflicts we experience in and around our work are derived from the chains of interdependencies in which we live; it is our fate to be involved in them. We are social animals; we simply can't avoid it.

Struggle for survival The second philosophy we need to investigate if we are to find out whether we are destined to be a rat is one I will call *biological*. Though it emerged in the nineteenth century, it still has a powerful influence on our lives.

The conflict we have with one another is aimed at survival and the need to procreate. As the biologist Richard Dawkins once said, we are nothing more than survival mechanisms for our genes. Whatever we do, we'll eventually be presented with the bill: was what we did beneficial for our survival and our

---

*Richard Sennett has written a revealing study about network organizations: *The Corrosion of Character: The personal consequences of work in the new capitalism*, Norton, 2000.

need to procreate or not? Much of our behavior is rooted in this biological soil: not just our tendency for cooperation, competition, and caring, but also our tendency to kill and commit genocide.

Competition is rife in the animal world, particularly between members of the same species. Conflicts erupt over territory, food, and mates. Every day the struggle for survival continues. All that hissing, humming, and growling is simply nature's rendition of "I will survive."

The way in which this struggle finds expression varies from one species to another, and even within the same species. Animals chase each other away or threaten each other. Males stage ritual dances to decide who will claim the waiting female. Like wolves, packs band together to fight other packs. They wound; they fight to the death.

Are we nothing more than a violent, collusive ape? Opinions differ. Some books suggest we are; others protest that we are really quite nice creatures.

But what does Darwin's theory mean for the political power games in our companies? Should we assume that anybody who plays a dirty trick, or undermines a manager, or strives to make it before they hit 40, is simply struggling for survival and fighting to pass on their genes? Could it be that the backstabbing, the gossip, the character assassination, the kicking upstairs, the coups, the takeovers, and the endless strife are no more than scenes from nature's cruel script?

Are human beings no more than bags of warm water, protein, and bone? If they are, our political game is merely biological programming. All we can do is bow our heads in humility and say: I'm a foul, vicious rat; there's nothing I can do about it.

Being I'd like to discuss one last school of thought that leads the rat on to a *philosophical* stage. We're dealing here with nothing less than the nature of being itself. Is it a physical, chemical, biological, or social reality? Is there a factor at work here that's been active ever since the Big Bang?

And so we arrive at Friedrich Nietzsche, the nineteenth-century philosopher who concerned himself with such matters.* His observations shed a light on the rat that is both exciting and discomfiting. Nietzsche is at odds with our liberal and humane ideas about professional behavior.

Although Nietzsche was opposed to investigating the nature of being, he couldn't help doing so. He identifies one factor that is always at work: the desire for power. It's a force that propels everything in nature and human life. As he wrote in one of his later works, *Beyond Good and Evil*:

"It must be the desire for power, it wishes to grow, to enlarge, to attract, to gain supremacy—not on the grounds of morality or immorality, but because it is alive and because life itself is the desire for power."

No matter what we do, the desire for power is present in everything that happens:

"Imagine, finally, that we could succeed in explaining all our passions as the branches and tributaries of one fundamental urge—the desire for power, as I maintain in my thesis; imagine that all organizational functions can be attributed to this desire for power and in this could be found the solution to the problem of procreation and feeding—for they are one problem—then one would have earned the right to define all active forces as one single force: the desire for power. The internal world, the world

---

*I'd like to point you to *Nietzsche: A philosophical biography*, Norton, 2003, a subtle monograph by the German philosopher Rudiger Safranski. He is a true teacher; he provides access to a tradition.

defined and typified according to its "intelligible character"—
would be nothing more than the desire for power."

Note that the quotation is couched in hypothetical terms.
Nietzsche leaves himself room for maneuver.

In *Thus Spake Zarathustra*, another of his philosophical
works, the caution has gone. Observe how he describes life
itself: "That I have to be struggle, and becoming, and purpose,
and cross-purpose—ah, he who divineth my will, divineth well
also on what crooked paths it hath to tread!"*

Life itself claims a will of its own. What that will is remains
for us to decide. But it is the desire for power. And what does he
mean by *crooked* roads? Nothing more than that power makes
strange moves to realize itself. Loving people? Nothing more
than a crooked path by which to attain power. Generosity,
morals? Nothing other than power. Everything is power,
because the desire for power is Being.

Enough quotations. Let's now return to our basic everyday
corporate theme: how do I screw my adversary? How can I be a rat?

It's interesting to speculate what Nietzsche would have
thought of the way people operate in organizations. He'd
probably have argued that companies in today's global market
economy are nothing more than crooked paths engineered by
the desire for power. In our offices, our meetings, our change
interventions, our open collaborations and secret collusions, we
walk to the rhythm of our desire for power. And we should cast
a suspicious eye on liberal working methods, inspiring
leadership, and participatory approaches: here the desire for
power may be particularly rampant.

So, if you are a rat, you do no more than follow your most
basic instincts. You embody in all your friendliness and

---

*E-book edition, translated by Thomas Common, eBookMall, 2000.

viciousness, your overt strategies and your devious calculations, nothing other than the desire for power. Thanks to Nietzsche, you are now officially recognized as an asshole.

I've shown you a few excerpts from the tradition because every vicious trick you use has its roots and its forefathers. What do we owe to tradition?

First, we owe a debt of gratitude to the people who gave us the terminology and the models to draw a line between politics and the normal flow of life. We saw how discussions about power and its games can take place only against the backdrop of larger social groups: cities. We saw too how the struggle for power isn't confined to actual violence, but includes all sorts of manipulative techniques that we still use today: rhetoric. Then we took a closer look at an important aspect of power: the power to reduce another person's options. The early Christian Church was particularly skilled at this.

The Renaissance taught us about the craft of the power game. In an amoral and down-to-earth way, Machiavelli gave us the first power cookbook. We are grateful to the eighteenth and nineteenth centuries for the repertoire of "Big Brother" repression measures. From now on, we can separate the pure from the impure, and cleanse it or dispose of it. And finally we investigated the claim that all is conflict. We looked at conflict in three different ways: first, as a consequence of chains of social interdependencies; second, as a biological struggle for survival; and third, as an expression of the desire for power that works through everything—physical, biological, and social.

When you play a trick, you sing from the songbook written by sociology, biology, or philosophy.

Time for the epilogue.

Epilogue

The house is in one of those crowded developments. It's almost impossible to reach it by car. A kid on one of those superaerodynamic scooters nearly goes under my wheels. Shit. I'm in a hurry. It's planned for 2:15. Here it is. Thank goodness the weather's fine. June. That's nice for the family. Is the family going to be there? Oh yes—just a son and a daughter.

I park my car and check my bag. At least the poison is still cool. I've brought some extra needles. The last time it went wrong. Disaster. They even had to call in the inspector of euthanasia. And I've been doing this work for years. Never had a complaint before. Not one. Until then. Terrible.

This must be it. Normal house. Nothing special. Front yard a bit overgrown. Needs seeing to. I double-check the bar code my colleague has stuck on the door. Yes. This is it. I knock. The door opens.

That must be the daughter. I recognize the broad forehead from the photo. Nowadays they send a photo of the victim with the email. Started doing that when there was a mix-up up north. Her eyes are red from weeping. Mascara is running down her face. Didn't she read my tips for those who are attending at a euthanasia? It says quite clearly: no makeup, comfortable clothes, no alcohol.

"Come in," she sighs.

I enter. The hall is gloomy. We go into a room. The curtains are half-closed. There is a deep, pregnant silence. The sickly smell of cauliflower. Jesus Christ. I told them to burn some incense. I'll never get used to that smell. I feel queasy: rotting. The patient is lying in the parlor. I can see the foot of the bed through the door. I hear soft voices.

I gesture to the daughter to go in first. I don't want anybody looking over my shoulder while I prepare my things. Only makes them nervous. Nowadays we use hygienic pistols. You hold them on the arm and the needle automatically finds an artery and injects the poison. Very handy. Very neat. You used to have to do it all yourself. That was nasty: all the family sitting around while you searched for the right spot. I do a final check: needles, OK. Poison, OK. Papers, OK. Well then, here we go.

I walk into the front room and find an elderly lady lying there. Half sitting up, as we had instructed. The son and daughter are holding her hands. They've also put on the plastic bib. Sometimes, just before it happens, they vomit. Makes a terrible mess.

The daughter makes room for me so that I can reach. As I sit down, everyone is silent. They look at me expectantly. The old woman's eyes are glowing from the morphine. The daughter's makeup is ruined. The son is keeping a stiff upper lip. I sit down because I'm sure the old woman will want to say something.

She smiles. At me, at her daughter, at her son, and then at me again. Her face tightens. She gives me a penetrating look.

"You were there. You were in Auschwitz. In Jerusalem. In Belfast. In New York." She stops for a moment and swallows.

"You were there, weren't you?"

Puzzling words from a woman I've never seen before in my life. The daughter sobs. The son can hardly control himself.

"Shall we, then?" I ask.

The old woman nods.

I take her arm and attach the pistol. She feels very warm. I look at her, as they taught us to do in training. A friendly face, innocence itself. I will be the last person she sees. The birds sing. Somewhere in the distance, the sound of an electric drill. The longest day can begin.

174

EPILOGUE

And then I begin to count to myself: three, two, one ...

About the author

Joep Schrijvers has written numerous articles about personal development, coaching, and learning. He has worked as a researcher, trainer, video director, manager, and consultant, and now lectures and writes about corporate politics, irrational behavior, and the role of chance in change processes. He has a special interest in corporate narratives, many of which have found their way into this book.